Psobriety

For those still struggling to break free from the prison of alcoholism and addiction.

> Then they cried to the LORD in their trouble,
>   and he saved them from their distress;
> he brought them out of darkness and gloom,
>   and broke their bonds asunder.
> Let them thank the LORD for his steadfast love,
>   for his wonderful works to humankind.
> For he shatters the doors of bronze,
>   and cuts in two the bars of iron.
>   (Psalm 107:13–16)

Psobriety

A Journey of Recovery through the Psalms

Jeff Dafler

WESTMINSTER
JOHN KNOX PRESS
LOUISVILLE · KENTUCKY

© 2021 Jeff Dafler

First Edition
Published by Westminster John Knox Press
Louisville, Kentucky

21 22 23 24 25 26 27 28 29 30—10 9 8 7 6 5 4 3 2 1

Unless otherwise indicated, Scripture quotations are from the New Revised Standard Version of the Bible, copyright © 1989 by the Division of Christian Education of the National Council of the Churches of Christ in the U.S.A., and are used by permission.

Excerpts from the "Big Book" or "Big Book of Alcoholics Anonymous" are from W., Bill. *Alcoholics Anonymous: The Story of How Many Thousands of Men and Women Have Recovered from Alcoholism.* New York: Alcoholics Anonymous World Services, 1976. Excerpts from Tom Petty and the Heartbreakers, "The Waiting," recorded April 30, 1981, track 1 on *Hard Promises*, Backstreet Records BSR-5160, 33 1/3 rpm. Excerpt from Kansas, "Dust in the Wind," by Kerry Livgren, recorded October 17, 1978, *Dust in the Wind*, D. Kirshner Music, single. Excerpts from Seldom Scene, "Working on a Building," recorded at the Kennedy Center, November 10, 1986, side D, track 1 on *The Seldom Scene 15th Anniversary Celebration*, Sugar Hill SH-2202, 12 inch.

Book design by Sharon Adams
Cover design by Mary Ann Smith

Library of Congress Cataloging-in-Publication Data is on file at the Library of Congress, Washington DC.

ISBN-13: 978-0-664-26696-7

Most Westminster John Knox Press books are available at special quantity discounts when purchased in bulk by corporations, organizations, and special-interest groups. For more information, please e-mail SpecialSales@wjkbooks.com.

Contents

Introduction

The book of Psalms has always been close to the heart of my spirituality. Whether near or far from a Higher Power, I turned to the Psalms at various points throughout my life as I searched for truth, freedom, and hope. So, when I finally decided to get serious about sobriety, I returned to this spectacular collection of Hebrew poetry to help sustain me on my journey of recovery.

On my first day of sobriety, an idea occurred to me that would help see me through my first five months without a drink—read one psalm each morning. Simple, right? But what a precious gift this was! As I worked my way through the book, while also beginning my work on the Twelve Steps of Alcoholics Anonymous, I found the full range of emotions that I was feeling and experiencing: fear, hope, struggle, praise, thanksgiving, anger, loss, compassion, humility, and victory.

These beautiful, stirring songs of faith bolstered my resolve, channeled my anguish, and comforted me. They gave voice to my soul, which, especially in that first month without a drink, was often too broken to speak for itself. Sometimes I cried, sometimes I laughed, but I kept coming back to them every morning. And there, in those words, I gradually found the God of my liberation.

I write this book with the newcomer in mind, but I hope the readings might be of value to anyone in recovery. I write specifically about my experience with alcohol, my drug of choice, but the Psalms can be a wellspring of hope for anyone who wants to break free from the shackles of addiction. While the substances we turned to as a solution to our problems might differ, we share a common bond in the hopelessness and despair we felt while in the grip of our disease—and the healing that awaits us when we accept our own powerlessness over alcohol or drugs and lean into the strength of a Higher Power.

About the Psalms

The Psalms originated as holy texts of the Jewish faith and became an integral part of the Christian canon. While I am a Christian, I have a deep respect for all faiths and the foundational principle of Alcoholics Anonymous that each one of us must build a personal relationship with the God *of our own understanding*. This book is not an endorsement of any one religion, denomination, sect, or creed over another, but simply a tool for those who seek to improve conscious contact with a power greater than themselves, as the eleventh step of the program of Alcoholics Anonymous suggests that we should do. Throughout these devotions, you will notice I use "God," "God of our understanding," and "Higher Power" interchangeably, as is common in many recovery programs. These terms are intended to be inclusive of any particular understanding of a power greater than ourselves that can help us develop and maintain a sober way of living.

In the first three words of Psalm 1, "Happy are those," we get right to the point of the book of Psalms. At their core, the Psalms provide a compelling guide to happy, God-centered living. These beautiful poems collectively suggest a set of principles that share a remarkable consistency with the steps of recovery outlined in the program of Alcoholics Anonymous. They call us to recognize and accept a Higher Power as the creator who is in charge of all things. We must submit our will to this Higher Power, learn God's teachings and live in harmony with God's plan for our lives.

When we follow this path, we will experience joy, freedom, strength, and peace. When we choose our own way over God's, things tend not to turn out so well. As a whole, the Psalms describe the striving of individuals and the broader community to live in faithful response to this Higher Power. The terms "righteousness" and "wickedness" are often used to describe what life looks like when lived in sync (righteousness) and out of sync (wickedness) with God and God's teachings or will. In the simplest of terms, righteous living, which for this alcoholic equates entirely with sober living, begins with acknowledgment that God is in control. The righteous are those who see God as the all-powerful source of everything good and seek to stay close to God, trying more each day to follow God's will and way for their lives.

The psalmists also readily admit that while God is perfect, we are not. Many of the Psalms include the anguished cries of those who have fallen short in their efforts to live in harmony with God's teachings. Bad things happen to good people, and good people sometimes do bad things. The psalmists, like all of us, try to take control back from their Higher Power and run their lives into the ditch. They suffer the pain of attempting to live life on their own terms and call out to the God of their understanding for rescue, forgiveness, comfort, and guidance. Their honesty and openness can be breathtaking in their celebration of God's good gifts, and gut-wrenching in their portrayal of the pain of human tragedy. Across the full range of victory and loss they describe, however, we see God hear their cries and restore them to physical, emotional, and spiritual health, setting them back on the righteous path that leads to happiness. God gives them the hope and strength they could never find alone, bringing them together in community to love and support one another. The God of the Psalms is always and forever the God of recovery.

About the Readings

Each of the following 150 readings is based on the corresponding psalm from the Bible. I recommend that you read one each day as part of your time of reflection and meditation. Each reading begins with a brief, one- or two-verse passage from the day's psalm, but I suggest reading the whole psalm for that day. In many Christian Bibles they can be found near the middle, or you can pull the Psalms up on a Bible app or Bible website. The verses quoted in this book are taken from the New Revised Standard Version (NRSV) of the Bible, but you can choose whatever translation suits you. Just be aware that there could be some minor wording differences between the translation you are reading and the NRSV quotations in this book.

After reading the psalm, prayerfully pause before moving to the corresponding daily reflection for that psalm. In the reading for each day, I reflect on the challenges of sobriety and how the Psalms offer wisdom for those in recovery. I share stories from my own journey and principles I have learned from the program and fellowship of Alcoholics Anonymous. I draw heavily from the book *Alcoholics Anonymous*, affectionately known as the "Big Book" in AA circles, the *Twelve Steps and Twelve Traditions*, and the pamphlet the *Four Absolutes*.

I am not a biblical scholar, and there are certainly many people who know more about twelve-step recovery programs than I do. One of the important lessons I must learn as a recovering alcoholic is that I do not and cannot know everything. What I have also learned is that sharing my experience, strength, and hope with other alcoholics and addicts is important to maintaining my own sobriety. These writings are offered in that spirit.

At the end of each daily reflection is a suggested prayer. You can pray it silently to yourself or out loud. I am fairly confident your Higher Power will hear it either way! Each prayer ends with a request that God will keep us sober today. I believe there is no more important prayer for an alcoholic or addict.

The Daily Readings

Psalm 1

Happy are those
  who do not follow the advice of the wicked,
or take the path that sinners tread,
  or sit in the seat of scoffers;
but their delight is in the law of the LORD,
  and on his law they meditate day and night.

(vv. 1–2)

This first psalm begins with a powerful word: Happy! How elusive happiness seemed on my first day without alcohol. I was very sick—physically, emotionally, and spiritually. My hands were shaking, my head throbbing, my stomach churning. I had lost my job, badly hurt the people who loved me most, and turned my back on the very idea of a Higher Power. I was broken, alone, and filled with despair.

I felt miles away from anything even remotely close to happy. Yet in the first words of the psalm, "Happy are those," was a glimmer of hope. There *are* those in the world who are happy. I saw them at an AA meeting I went to the evening of that first day without a drink. And I desperately wanted to feel what they felt.

There in verse 2 was a clue that I didn't fully understand yet. Those happy people find their delight in meditating on God's teachings "day and night." At this point, I was willing to try anything to stop the pain. So, I started reading a psalm, a section from the Big Book, and praying every day. It was the first step in a long journey of recovery. A journey toward happiness.

God of happy people, thank you for giving us a glimpse of a better way. Please keep us sober today.

Psalm 2

I will tell of the decree of the LORD:
He said to me, "You are my son;
   today I have begotten you.
Ask of me, and I will make the nations your heritage,
   and the ends of the earth your possession."

(vv. 7–8)

This psalm opens with earthly rulers plotting and planning ways to increase their power and control. For years, I thought I had to control everything and everyone in my life. I obsessed over it almost constantly, full of anxiety and fear that my carefully crafted plans would fall apart, that my plots would be in vain, as verse 1 says.

The more I tried—and failed—to control things, the more I drank. Sometimes I drank to calm my anxiety and quiet my racing mind. Other times I drank to console myself when my grand schemes fell apart. Like many addicts and alcoholics, I found only temporary relief. Alcohol and drugs might give us a momentary escape from troubles of our own making, but they always make things worse in the long run.

In Psalm 2, we read a magnificent promise from God: "You are my child; today I have begotten you." This God, our Father, has all power. No longer do we need to worry or be afraid, no longer do we need to plot in vain. The God of the Psalms invites us to find our rest and refuge in him. All we have to do is let go.

All-powerful Creator, thank you for making us your children. Help us to let go of our need to control everything, and instead, turn it over to you. Please keep us sober today.

Psalm 3

I cry aloud to the LORD,
    and he answers me from his holy hill.

. . . .

I am not afraid of ten thousands of people
    who have set themselves against me all around.

(vv. 4, 6)

When we first stop drinking and using, it can feel as if the whole world is conspiring against us like the foes in Psalm 3. Old friends want us to go out and party. Every commercial on television seems to be about alcohol. Even that little voice inside is saying, "Come on! Just one. No one will know!"

Sitting in my first AA meeting, I started thinking about two bottles of beer I still had at home in the fridge (I had drunk everything else). I thought maybe I should just polish those off when I got home, and *then* I would quit. I mean, I already paid for them, right?

As the meeting ended, a nice couple came up to me, introduced themselves and told me they were glad I had come. They said all I could do was just not drink, one day at a time. And then, the woman gave me a "healing spirit" coin with a small prayer on the back.

When I got home, I prayed the prayer on that coin and repeated the small prayer I had said the day before: "God, please help me!" Somehow, God answered my prayer. I felt a rush of strength come over me. I went to the fridge, got the two bottles of beer, opened them, and poured them down the sink. To me, that was evidence that God has the power to defeat alcohol, my biggest enemy.

All-powerful God, thank you for saving us from our relentless foe. Please keep us sober today.

Psalm 4

You have put gladness in my heart
  more than when their grain and wine abound.
I will both lie down and sleep in peace;
  for you alone, O Lord, make me lie down in safety.

(vv. 7–8)

The psalmist here is suffering some ongoing trouble and asking God to rescue him. It would be nice if all our problems would disappear when we stopped drinking and using, but that's not usually how it works.

For most of us, the lies we told, the hurt we caused, and the damage we did—to ourselves and others—weren't magically wiped out when we put down the bottle. We come to realize that years of destructive behavior take a long time to overcome.

We learn to accept, though, that those wounds can only heal if we stop doing more harm. Getting drunk, getting high, no matter how badly we might want to, would only make things worse. We must begin to trust that the happiness that comes from our Higher Power is greater than when the "grain and wine abound." And, God won't give us a hangover!

Help us to turn to you, God, instead of the bottle when the urge to drink or use hits. May we sleep in peace knowing that you will never abandon us. Please keep us sober today.

Psalm 5

Lead me, O LORD, in your righteousness
    because of my enemies;
    make your way straight before me.
For there is no truth in their mouths;
    their hearts are destruction

(vv. 8-9a)

There are many voices trying to tell us there is an easier, softer way than the Twelve Steps and total reliance on a power greater than ourselves. These may be the voices of our friends or the people with whom we used to drink or use. They may be the voices of enablers who made excuses for us and tried to protect us from the consequences of our addiction. For me, the voices came mostly from within.

We learn from the Big Book that alcohol (like any drug) is cunning, baffling, and powerful. Once it has us in its grasp, it doesn't want to let us go. The good news is that there is a power greater than alcohol or drugs—a power that can "cast them out," as the psalmist writes in today's poem.

I found that the more meetings I attended, the more I prayed, the more I read the Big Book and surrounded myself with sober people, the quieter those voices became. I doubt they will ever leave me for good, but I hear them less frequently with each passing day. If I turn to my Higher Power for help and listen for this voice alone, whether in the words of a psalm or the encouragement of a friend in recovery, I can stay sober one more day.

God, we ask that you would silence the voices that call us back to misery and despair. May we listen only for your voice calling us to a life of freedom, peace, and joy. Please keep us sober today.

Psalm 6

Be gracious to me, O LORD, for I am languishing;
O LORD, heal me, for my bones are shaking with
terror.

(v. 2)

We learn in "The Doctor's Opinion" at the beginning of the Big
Book of Alcoholics Anonymous that we suffer from a disease. In
his letter, Dr. William Silkworth writes about his experience trying to treat the disease of alcoholism, its symptoms and causes,
as well as his frustration with various methods and failed "cures."
As with the writer of Psalm 6, Dr. Silkworth came to believe
that only God has the power to save us from our suffering. Many
of us alcoholics and addicts have tried without success to control our disease on our own. Perhaps we tried to moderate our
intake. I tried switching to only beer and wine, tried to drink only
on weekends, only in the evening, only after noon. None of it
seemed to work for long. When we finally face the evidence, we
must accept that we are powerless over alcohol and drugs—that
our disease has made our lives unmanageable.

But as we begin to recover, we come to believe that there is
One who has all power, One who will not leave us to languish
in our disease forever, One who will hear our pleas and heal us.
That One is God. Cry out—God will answer.

*Loving God, the Great Physician, begin your healing work in us
now. We are suffering from the disease of addiction, but we trust
that you have the power to make us well. We pray that you will
keep us sober today.*

Psalm 7

God is my shield,
> who saves the upright in heart.
>> (v. 10)

As I meditate on the Psalms over time, they reveal insights into the trouble that arises when I live according to my own will instead of God's plan for my life. Reading Psalm 7 in very early sobriety, it drove home the truth of how my addiction led me to mischief and lies, how we alcoholics and addicts "make a pit, digging it out, and fall into the hole that [we] have made" (v. 15).

These realizations of the truth of our past behavior can be painful. As we emerge gradually from the haze of addiction, we begin to see that we were often our own worst enemies. We can begin to admit our wrongs and accept that, fueled by drink or drugs, we caused so much pain and damage to ourselves and others.

It is important for each of us to acknowledge and accept the truth about who we are. It is equally important to acknowledge and accept the truth about who our Higher Power made us to be. If we can turn from our old ways of thinking and living, if we can put our trust not in our own power but in the power of One greater than ourselves, there is hope for a better life.

"God is my shield" (v. 10). When I turn and place my trust in God, through prayer and working the steps, God will protect me and bless me with a new life in sobriety. God will forgive my wrongs and grant me a new freedom and a new happiness.

God of new beginnings, give us eyes to see ourselves as we are and hearts to trust in your promise of a better life. Please keep us sober today.

Psalm 8

When I look at your heavens, the work of your fingers,
   the moon and the stars that you have established;
what are human beings that you are mindful of them,
   mortals that you care for them?
Yet you have made them a little lower than God,
   and crowned them with glory and honor.

(vv. 3–5)

The God of my understanding is the One who has all power—the source of all that exists, a caring, loving creator. When I take in the magical beauty of the moon and stars early on a cold, clear morning, I am amazed that God also made me.

I am reminded of the way I've heard the Lord's Prayer introduced at the end of a few AA meetings: "Who hung the stars and keeps us out of bars? Our Father . . ."

I have heard quite a few fellow AAs say that their old concept of a Higher Power, often developed in childhood, was of an angry, punishing God. That's not the God they ended up knowing after working the steps, nor is it the God of Psalm 8. The poet writes instead of a loving creator who made us "a little lower than God" (v. 5).

God doesn't want us to be slaves to alcohol or drugs. No, God loves us so much that he wants a better life for us. He loves us enough to break the chains of addiction and lead us on a journey of recovery to a life that is happy, joyous, and free!

Creator of the universe and all that is in it, thank you for loving us enough to free us from the slavery of addiction. Please give us the strength to do the work of recovery and keep us sober today.

Psalm 9

The LORD is a stronghold for the oppressed,
　　a stronghold in times of trouble.
And those who know your name put their trust in you,
　　for you, O LORD, have not forsaken those who seek you.
(vv. 9–10)

As we near the end of our drinking and using, our powerlessness over our substance of choice becomes ever more difficult to deny. For much of my life, booze was my go-to solution. Whenever I needed to feel better, to escape and hide from stress, anxiety, and fear, a bottle was there.

Eventually, though, I lost choice in the matter as the solution became part of the problem. No longer did I drink because I wanted to or because it made me feel better. I drank because I had to. Alcohol had taken control!

No matter what I tried, I found I didn't have the power to control my drinking. I felt like one of the "oppressed" we read about in Psalm 9. I was in desperate need of refuge, and like the psalmist, I gradually found a safe haven in my Higher Power.

For so long, when things got rough, I took a drink—or twenty. As I began my sobriety journey, I had to learn to turn to a God of my own understanding. I had to begin to place my trust in God as the only stronghold that could keep me sober and take away my fears. I began to learn that the more willing I become to hand things over to God, the more God's power can flow through me.

Wonderful God, may we learn to trust in you more every day. You are the One who has all power. Be our refuge in times of trouble, and please keep us sober today.

Psalm 10

O Lord, you will hear the desire of the meek;
    you will strengthen their heart, you will incline your ear
to do justice for the orphan and the oppressed,
    so that those from earth may strike terror no more.

(vv. 17–18)

Learning to trust God can be hard in early sobriety. As alcoholics and addicts, patience is seldom our strong suit, and, like the psalmist, we may get the feeling that God is standing far off (v. 1). We typically want results and want them now! When we stop drinking and using, we soon realize that the rest of the world continues much in the way it had before. Old friends continue living in ways we are trying to leave behind. The things that need to be fixed in our lives or in the world still need fixing.

To stay sober, though, we must let these things go and turn them over to our Higher Power. Psalm 10 assures us that God is listening, ready to strengthen us and soothe our fears (vv. 17–18). We must learn to trust that the God of our understanding can and will handle things beyond our control. But we must also accept that this God works in his own time, in his own way.

Sometimes God's way will be slower than our way, different than our way. If we stop and think about it, though, how did doing things our own way work out for us? For those we love? Sure, we likely had our share of success in life, but ultimately our own way usually took us to the bottom of a bottle.

God's way will lead us to a better life. God's way is the way of hope, joy, love, and peace. We must trust that if we are patient and work the steps, God will take care of the rest.

All-powerful God, help us to trust you more and to wait patiently for the better life you have in store for us. Please keep us sober today.

16

Psalm 11

In the LORD I take refuge; how can you say to me,
"Flee like a bird to the mountains."

(v. 1)

Sometimes our old life—certainly our disease—doesn't want to let us go. Some of us lived many years as drunks or addicts. The people around us who know our histories can sometimes be skeptical about our ability to change. Others might be like the person telling the psalmist to "flee like a bird to the mountains," encouraging us to try to manage things ourselves instead of turning to God and a program of recovery.

But at recovery meetings we find people willing to tell us the truth—about themselves and about addiction. We can relate to their stories of drinking, using, powerlessness and defeat. In recovery programs, we finally can begin to feel like we belong, like we have found people who understand our struggles—people who have discovered a real solution that has transformed their lives.

Recovery meetings can quickly become our refuge, and there we can find a Higher Power speaking to us through our fellow alcoholics and addicts. The more we listen and the more we try to do what they are doing, the more those other voices of defeat and despair fade away.

God, help us to keep coming back to the refuge of the recovery community where we can find strength and hope to live the life you have in store for us. Please keep us sober today.

Psalm 12

The promises of the LORD are promises that are pure,
   silver refined in a furnace on the ground,
   purified seven times.
You, O LORD, will protect us;
   you will guard us from this generation forever.

(vv. 6–7)

I'm reminded of an AA saying I first heard a couple of weeks after I started going to meetings: "Never forget that our disease is out in the parking lot doing push-ups." Indeed, it can often feel as if wickedness is prowling on every side, as the author of Psalm 12 writes, especially when we first get sober.

I used to be one of those people who believe "with our tongues we will prevail," as it says in verse 4. I thought I could talk my way out of any jam. Eventually, though, the jams got bigger and more frequent until that's all there was. Life became nothing but an endless stream of trouble flowing straight out of the bottle.

That's how it was when we were drinking and using, when we had convinced ourselves we were in charge and could handle anything. Yet all the while, a substance was our master, demanding we turn over ever more control.

When our disease has finally beaten us into a state of reasonableness, as it says in the Big Book of Alcoholics Anonymous (p. 48), and we can honestly admit our powerlessness over alcohol or drugs, then our Higher Power can finally begin to work in our lives. We come to find that God's promises are pure, and that God can and will protect and guard us, one day at a time.

O God, we ask your protection today. Our disease is strong, but we know you are stronger. Please keep us sober today.

Psalm 13

How long, O LORD? Will you forget me forever?
How long will you hide your face from me?
How long must I bear pain in my soul,
and have sorrow in my heart all day long?
How long shall my enemy be exalted over me?

(vv. 1–2)

Patience was never my strong suit, and I have learned many of my fellow alcoholics and addicts share that shortcoming. I wanted it all, and I wanted it now! It seems the author of Psalm 13 can feel our pain.

During the first few weeks of sobriety, we are often desperate to feel better. We want to stop shaking, stop running to the bathroom, stop the pounding in our heads. As the physical pain begins to fade, we are still emotionally and psychologically broken. We may be thankful that we're not drinking or using, but our hearts still echo the words in verse 2. How long would we bear the pain and sorrow?

I remember hearing someone in a discussion meeting say that SOBER is an acronym for "Son of a Bitch, Everything's Real!" I laughed out loud because it rang so true for me. For years, alcohol was my coping mechanism. But over time that solution became an uncontrollable problem. Now I had to learn how to live life on life's own terms.

I also had to accept that wouldn't happen overnight. I had to begin living on God's time, not my time, and God's time is one day at a time. Gradually, I discovered that if I did the right thing today—go to meetings, pray, read the Big Book, get a sponsor, work the steps—that my Higher Power would take care of tomorrow.

God, grant us the patience to focus on today and the faith to turn tomorrow over to you. Please keep us sober today.

Psalm 14

Fools say in their hearts, "There is no God."
   They are corrupt, they do abominable deeds;
   there is no one who does good.
The LORD looks down from heaven on humankind
   to see if there are any who are wise,
   who seek after God.

                                   (vv. 1–2)

The "God thing" can be a stumbling block for many of us when we first try to get help. Whether we're atheists, agnostics, or people who have had a bad or very little prior experience with organized religion, we can be uncomfortable with—even downright hostile to—the spirituality that infuses many recovery programs.

When I first tried AA, the group prayers and references to a Higher Power and God turned me off. It became my excuse for not going back, and I decided to try controlling my drinking on my own. Of course, I was soon drinking more than ever as my life continued to implode.

I finally became so desperate that I was willing to try anything, even the "God thing" that I so despised. I read the chapter "We Agnostics" in the Big Book one day, and I had one of those "moments of clarity" I hear people talk about. I suddenly realized why the author of Psalm 14 declares it's a fool who says, "There is no God."

If we deny the existence of a Higher Power, we are closing ourselves off to new possibilities. Many of us tried to quit drinking and using on our own, but our power, by itself, was never enough. The good news awaiting us in recovery, though, is we don't have to do this alone. When we "seek after him," God will do for us what we could not do for ourselves.

Thank you, God, for never giving up on us, even when we give up on you. We humbly ask you to please keep us sober today.

Psalm 15

O Lord, who may abide in your tent?
Who may dwell on your holy hill?
Those who walk blamelessly, and do what is right,
and speak the truth from their heart.

(vv. 1–2)

When we first embark on our journey of recovery, it can be difficult to see beyond the immediate mess our lives likely have become thanks to our addiction. The desire to stop drinking or using is about the only goal we might be able to muster for quite a while. Even early on, though, we begin to see that the sober people we encounter have something we want. And we often hear them say, "If you want what we have, then do what we did."

Psalm 15 lays out a solid foundation for the work that lies before us. The writer asks in the opening verse what God would have us do. We can easily see some core recovery principles in verses 2–4:

- "Walk blamelessly and do what is right." (Do the next right thing.)
- "Speak the truth from [the] heart." (Rigorous honesty.)
- "Do not slander . . . do no evil to . . . friends and neighbors." (Love others and forgive.)
- "Do not lend money at interest . . . do not take a bribe against the innocent." (Be unselfish.)

These instructions are a close reflection of Alcoholics Anonymous' Four Absolutes: honesty, unselfishness, love, and purity. For most of us, these principles represent a new way of living. And they are the key to our sobriety. As God promises at the conclusion of the psalm, if we live accordingly, we "shall never be moved."

God, you have granted us the priceless gift of sobriety. May we respond by living according to your will for us. Please keep us sober today.

21

Psalm 16

Therefore my heart is glad, and my soul rejoices;
   my body also rests secure.
For you do not give me up to Sheol,
   or let your faithful one see the Pit.

(vv. 9–10)

Sometimes words of hope and assurance come when we most need them. We can turn to Psalm 16 when we feel weak and receive God's promise echoing the words of the Big Book of Alcoholics Anonymous: There is a solution!

We suffered from a sickness of the mind, body, and soul. Many of us tried to treat it for years with alcohol or drugs, and for a time it may have worked. Eventually, though, our chemical solution becomes an even worse problem. It becomes our god, controlling our thoughts and actions. We are living proof of the psalmist's claim in verse 4: "Those who choose another God multiply their sorrows."

But today, by the grace of God, we are living testimonies that there really is a solution! We have discovered that if we keep the God of our understanding "at my right hand," we can be restored to sanity. God will remove from us the obsession with alcohol or drugs and cause the boundary lines to fall in pleasant places for us, if only we embrace the spiritual heritage of the Twelve Steps that our predecessors in recovery have bequeathed to us.

If we put God first, work the steps and serve others, then indeed we will say with the psalmist, "my heart is glad, and my soul rejoices; my body also rests secure."

God, thank you for giving us a real solution and saving us from destruction and despair. Please keep us sober today.

Psalm 17

Guard me as the apple of the eye;
  hide me in the shadow of your wings.

(v. 8)

Many of the psalms seek divine deliverance from enemies who pursue the writer's destruction. Usually, these enemies are described as wicked people, but those of us in recovery face no bigger enemy than our own addiction.

In the rooms of Alcoholics Anonymous and other twelve-step programs, we sometimes hear our fellows personify this foe. I have often heard speakers remind me that I must never forget that our disease is lurking in the shadows, waiting to strike at the moment I stumble.

The author of Psalm 17 knows something about an enemy like ours. His enemy is tracking him down and surrounding him "like a lion eager to tear, like a young lion lurking in ambush (v. 12)." A realization like this can strike fear in our hearts and eat away at our serenity. What are we to do?

Instead of being paralyzed by fear of relapse, we can turn to the God of our understanding for protection. When we pray, attend meetings, work the Twelve Steps and try to be of service to others, we can share in the psalmist's confidence that our Higher Power will not let our enemy defeat us! As we practice these principles, we will find that God can transform our fear into faith.

God, guard us as the apple of your eye. Shelter us in the shadow of your mighty wings. Please keep us sober today.

Psalm 18

He brought me out into a broad place;
    he delivered me, because he delighted in me.

(v. 19)

In the personal stories of recovery that we read in books or hear at speaker meetings, others share with us what it used to be like, what happened, and what it's like now to live a sober life. In verses 4–19 of this psalm, we get David's story in a very similar pattern.

David shares his near hopeless state (vv. 4–5), entangled in the cords and snares of death and assailed on all sides. At his darkest moment, he cried out to his Higher Power, and God heard his voice. Then we read a beautiful poetic description of how God intervened to deliver David from an enemy that was too mighty for him to defeat on his own. At the end, God brings him out "into a broad place" (v. 19).

Sound familiar? In a few verses, Psalm 18 tells us all we need to know about beginning our journey of recovery. No matter how desperate or hopeless we feel, all we need to do is humbly, honestly admit our powerlessness and call out to our Higher Power for help. If we turn our will and our lives over to God's care, he will defeat our enemy and free us from our addiction. As we work the steps, we will gradually find ourselves delivered into the broad place of a sober, joyous life.

God, we cry out to you for help! Thank you for hearing our cry and leading us to a new life free from our enemy. Please keep us sober today.

Psalm 19

The law of the LORD is perfect,
    reviving the soul;
the decrees of the LORD are sure,
    making wise the simple;
the precepts of the LORD are right,
    rejoicing the heart;
the commandment of the LORD is clear,
    enlightening the eyes.

(vv. 7–8)

For many years, I clung to the dangerous idea that I made the rules. I was convinced of my uniqueness and believed I could—and must—bend the world to my will. The more tightly I held onto this false idea, the more frustration and disappointment I felt. As I built up my resentments and wallowed in self-pity, I began to drown myself in alcohol.

Psalm 19 tells us about a better way. If we let go of our old idea that we are in control and instead cling to our Higher Power's plan for our lives, things can and will get better. If we can honestly and fully embrace God's will for our lives, the psalmist tells us in verses 7 and 8 what is in store for us: God will revive our souls and make us wise. Our hearts will rejoice and we will (finally!) see clearly.

How priceless are such gifts! They are offered to us free of charge. All we have to do is follow this simple program for our lives. That program is laid out in the Psalms and in the Twelve Steps. In both versions, it starts with a basic acceptance that turns our old idea on its head: We can't. God can. We need to let him.

God, help us let go of our old ways and wrong ideas,
embracing instead your will and way for our lives. Please
keep us sober today.

25

Psalm 20

> May he grant you your heart's desire,
>   and fulfill all your plans.
> May we shout for joy over your victory,
>   and in the name of our God set up our banners.
> May the LORD fulfill all your petitions.
>
> (vv. 4–5)

Reading this psalm is like receiving assurances from the "old timers" at a twelve-step meeting. Part of the beauty of belonging to a community is that we no longer have to face everything alone. Instead, we are surrounded by people who genuinely understand what we have been through, because they have been through it too.

There is considerable diversity in the recovery fellowship. We will find people from every walk of life in the rooms of Alcoholics Anonymous and other twelve-step programs. I have formed friendships in AA with people I likely never would have even met or spoken to in the normal course of events. It turns out that what we share is far more significant than any differences in race, education, money, religion, or politics. Our disease does not discriminate!

These comrades in recovery want nothing more—and nothing less—for us than sobriety. They encourage us every day, as the psalmist does, to call on our Higher Power and trust that God will provide. They represent to us "the many victories" at God's right hand, living proof that "he will answer . . . from his holy heaven." Thanks to their example and encouragement, we come to believe a better life through sobriety is possible for every one of us.

God, thank you for surrounding us with people who can show us the path to sobriety and encourage us along the way. Please keep us sober today.

Psalm 21

He asked you for life; you gave it to him—
  length of days forever and ever.
His glory is great through your help;
  splendor and majesty you bestow on him.

(vv. 4–5)

This is a psalm of thanksgiving. Gratitude is definitely the attitude of enduring sobriety. For many people, being grateful is a natural response to the positives of daily life, but we alcoholics and addicts tend to dwell on the negatives.

Even when good things happened to me while I was still drinking, my perfectionism got in the way of lasting joy (and sometimes still does). If I achieved a goal at work, I would quickly think forward to the next rung on the ladder of success. If I lived in a nice house or drove a nice car, I would envy a neighbor's that were nicer still. I could never feel anything more than fleeting satisfaction or gratitude—and instead became increasingly critical of myself and resentful of others.

Gradually in sobriety, we come to feel a sense of thankfulness for the things God is doing for us that we could not do for ourselves. After a few weeks without a drink, I was grateful that I wasn't waking up in the fog of a hangover trying to piece together the previous night's events. I was thankful I wasn't shaking so badly that my handwriting was barely legible. It was a joy to be around people who seemed to care genuinely about me.

Most of all, I was thankful to have made it through another day without a drink. Like the king in Psalm 21, I had asked God for life, and God was giving it to me one day at a time. That was reason enough to give thanks!

Thank you, God, for the many gifts you have given us, none greater than sobriety. Please keep us sober one more day.

Lament. Prayer is a TOOL

Psalm 22

Deliver my soul from the sword,
   my life from the power of the dog!
Save me from the mouth of the lion!
From the horns of the wild oxen you have rescued me.

(vv. 20–21)

This psalm is clearly written by someone who is under threat. It opens with feelings of fear and urgency, even impatience that God seems slow to act. As the story unfolds, the psalmist remembers how God has saved him and the broader community in the past, all the way back to his own infancy and the very origins of his people. By the end, fear turns to faith as he imagines praising the Lord in the midst of the congregation and writes of God's coming victory.

Prayer is a powerful, transformative act. None of us is immune from fear, and life will always give us our fair share of sorrow and disappointments. Being sober doesn't mean we will no longer have to face hardships, but it does mean we don't have to face them alone—and we don't have to pick up a drink or drug. I'm reminded of the words of an old hymn, "What a Friend We Have in Jesus":

Have we trials and temptations?
Is there trouble anywhere?
We should never be discouraged,
Take it to the Lord in prayer.
(Joseph Scriven)

Often when feeling alone or afraid, I have begun praying to God for help. Never once have I failed to find some comfort and strength. The problems about which I pray are usually still there when I'm done, but the mere act of talking to God about them strengthens my faith, soothes my fears and restores my serenity.

God, we turn our troubles over to you. Thank you for giving us the strength and peace we need to handle whatever life throws our way. Please keep us sober today.

28

Psalm 23

The LORD is my shepherd, I shall not want.
   He makes me lie down in green pastures;
he leads me beside still waters;
   he restores my soul.
He leads me in right paths
   for his name's sake.

(vv. 1–3)

In the most famous of all the Psalms, we encounter God imagined as a shepherd. The psalmist paints a picture of what life is like when we are following God. It is a picture of serenity, harmony, comfort, abundance, and freedom from fear. It offers us a glimpse of the life awaiting us in sobriety if we are willing to do the work of recovery.

The focus of Psalm 23 is on God and the gifts he graciously bestows on each of us, but what is required of us? If our Higher Power is the shepherd, then we are the sheep. Our only job is to follow. If we faithfully do our job and follow the shepherd, then his care and protection will be ours.

For much of my life, though, I was not a very good sheep. I never felt like I belonged to the flock and tended to wander off into all kinds of trouble. A speaker at an AA meeting once described how shepherds sometimes broke the hind legs of lambs that kept getting lost from the flock. The shepherd would then carry the lamb around his neck and shoulders until its legs healed. After carrying around this once-wayward lamb, a close bond developed between human and animal. Not only was the lamb cured of its brokenness, but also of its desire to stray.

It is often like that with many of us. We keep wandering off on our own until our disease breaks us down. But our Higher Power is there to pick us up and carry us, helping us to heal and put our lives back together. There is no better shepherd.

God, thank you for rescuing us and bringing us back to the safety of your loving care. May we always follow you. Please keep us sober today.

Psalm 24

Who shall ascend the hill of the LORD?
  And who shall stand in his holy place?
Those who have clean hands and pure hearts,
  who do not lift up their souls to what is false,
  and do not swear deceitfully.

(vv. 3–4)

It is said that we suffer from a sickness of the mind, body, and soul. The antidote is learning to think and act differently, and the prescription is found in the Psalms and the Big Book of Alcoholics Anonymous.

All we need at the beginning is a little willingness and acceptance for God to begin his healing, transforming work in our lives. As we move forward one day at a time, we find we have some work to do, with God's help, to learn to live our lives on a different basis.

In verses 3 and 4 of Psalm 24, the psalmist asks what it takes to live into God's promise for our lives, and he provides an answer. He calls out two of AA's Four Absolutes: purity and honesty. It seems that purity can be a challenging concept to grasp. It does not mean "perfection," as even the authors of the Big Book readily admit they could not maintain "anything like perfect adherence" to AA's principles (p. 60). For me, purity is really a question of my motives. I have to examine closely *why* I am thinking or acting a certain way. Am I being manipulative, vindictive, or seeking to advance my own selfish interests? Or am I putting others first and genuinely trying to do good?

It is fitting that the psalmist pairs purity with honesty. We must be honest with God and ourselves to examine and discern if our motives are pure. Honesty with God makes honesty with others a much more achievable prospect.

God, we ask for the wisdom to start with pure motives and the courage to be honest when we miss the mark. Please keep us sober today.

Psalm 25

For your name's sake, O LORD,
pardon my guilt, for it is great.
Who are they that fear the LORD?
He will teach them the way that they should choose.

(vv. 11–12)

When I began my journey of recovery, I still carried a heavy weight. I knew in my heart that I had not been living a good life, and I was haunted by the harm I had done to myself and others while I was drinking.

We find in Psalm 25 a two-part prayer that begins with a plea for God's forgiveness. That plea is preceded by an honest acknowledgment of the psalmist's own wrongdoing. In recovery, it is through the fourth step that we come face-to-face with the truth of who we have been. If our personal inventory is truly "searching and fearless," it will allow us to honestly and humbly confess the exact nature of our wrongs to God, ourselves, and another person in our fifth step.

This "house cleaning," as it is known, is critical for at least two reasons. First, we suffer from a disease of perception. Much of our trouble had its root in our inability to see ourselves and the world as they truly were. If we can't get honest and see our own faults and limitations, it will be nearly impossible to avoid falling back into the same traps that led us to use in the first place.

Second, we will be unable to ask for and fully experience God's grace if we cannot embrace the honest humility of steps four and five. If we go to the doctor, we cannot expect healing if we are unable or unwilling to be honest and thorough in describing our symptoms. The same holds true with God, the great physician. We cannot receive God's gift of a beautiful life of sobriety unless we let go completely the burdens of the past.

God, help us find the honesty and courage to admit our wrongs so that we can experience the full release of your forgiveness. Please keep us sober today.

Psalm 26

But as for me, I walk in my integrity;
  redeem me, and be gracious to me.
My foot stands on level ground;
  in the great congregation I will bless the Lord.
                                                (vv. 11–12)

Have you ever heard the phrase, "Garbage in, garbage out?" It is often spoken in the context of the food we eat or things we consume and how they affect our health. As we read Psalm 26, however, we find a slightly different application of this truism.

Here we read the psalmist's testimony about not spending time with hypocrites and evildoers. Instead, he remains close to God's "altar" and spends time offering thanks on the "level ground" of God's congregation. In other words, he is staying away from the "garbage" that would pollute his mind and soul if he were spending time with the wrong people, places, and things. He chooses the company of God and the community of the faithful.

When I first came to Alcoholics Anonymous, I heard people talking about going to a meeting at least once a day for the first ninety days of sobriety. At first thought, this seemed extreme. Like much of the program, though, it ended up being a much more reasonable proposition if only I thought about it in more immediate terms. Could I make it to a meeting today? Yes, I could.

Over time, I found that answering that question in the affirmative, one day at a time, meant that I indeed ended up going to ninety meetings in ninety days. It meant that instead of putting more garbage into my mind and soul, I was spending more and more time filling up on the healing medicine God administered through the program and fellowship of AA. It meant I didn't have to take a drink today.

God, help us turn away from the garbage that pollutes our bodies, minds, and souls and fill up instead on the good things you offer. Please keep us sober today.

Psalm 27

I believe that I shall see the goodness of the LORD
   in the land of the living.
Wait for the LORD;
   be strong, and let your heart take courage;
   wait for the LORD!

                      (vv. 13–14)

The writer of Psalm 27 offers us a pattern for prayer that can be very effective. Often when I come to God in prayer, it is because I am troubled or fearful about something going on in my life. Like the author of this psalm, I seek my Higher Power's help, strength, and comfort.

The psalmist doesn't jump right into the request, though. He begins with an expression of his trust in God to protect him and provide for his needs. Why does this matter? I find when I pray this way, the mere act of praying itself begins the process of turning over to God that which I cannot control. It reminds me of the miraculous things that God has already done in my life and strengthens my faith that God will see me through any troubles I may face now or in the future.

When we embrace the psalmist's approach, we begin to learn something amazing as a result: Fear and faith cannot coexist. When we truly have faith that a Higher Power can and will save us, there is no room for fear in our hearts. This is part of what it means to be truly free. No longer must we allow fear to keep us in chains, controlling our thoughts and actions. Through faith in God's power, God will indeed grant us a new freedom and a new happiness. Our faith is strengthened, and our serenity grows, when we remind ourselves of this truth as we begin our prayers.

God, you have already worked miracles in our lives. May we have ever-growing faith in your power to free us from fear and despair. Please keep us sober today.

Psalm 28

Blessed be the LORD,
   for he has heard the sound of my pleadings.
The LORD is my strength and my shield;
   in him my heart trusts;
so I am helped, and my heart exults,
   and with my song I give thanks to him.

(vv. 6–7)

In the middle of Psalm 28, there is a plea for God to spare the psalmist from the fate of the "wicked." There is also the expression of an expectation: Those who do not turn to God, but rely instead on their own power, will reap what they sow. In other words, if we rely only on ourselves and live according to our own will, then we will get what we deserve.

This is a scary proposition. When I think about how I treated people while I was drinking, how I tried to manipulate them and use them to get what I wanted, I clearly do not deserve anything good in return. And for the most part, I was unable to get things to work in my favor when I was relying only on my own power. I could perhaps make things fall into place for a short while, but eventually everything would fall apart, despite my scheming. Then I would turn to the bottle to seek comfort, which also never seemed to last.

As the psalmist shows us, when instead we turn to God, however, he will protect us and give us what we need, even if it is not what our own selfish will desires. As it says in verse 7, it is by trusting the God of our understanding that we are helped. Once we decide to turn our will and our lives over to God's care, no longer must we scheme and plot. No longer will we be left to fend for ourselves because our Higher Power will be our strength and our shield.

God, be our strength and shield. Help us trust in you and know that you will give us all that we need. Please keep us sober today.

Psalm 29

The voice of the LORD is over the waters;
   the God of glory thunders,
   the LORD, over mighty waters.
The voice of the LORD is powerful;
   the voice of the LORD is full of majesty.

(vv. 3–4)

For much of my life, I had a belief in a powerless god, when I had any belief at all. I believed that this god might have been the source of the Big Bang that set the universe in motion, but he was otherwise a "hands-off" god who played no further role in the world of human affairs. Having arrived at a conception of a god who exercised no power, it was easy for me to ignore him altogether and grant myself license to try to control my life and those of the people around me.

Psalm 29 sings praise to an all-powerful God, different from the one many of us may have imagined. This is the God who speaks like thunder and rules over the mighty forces of nature. This is the God who gives his people strength and peace. This is also the God who hears our simple cry for help when our disease has stripped us of all other hope.

This God who "shakes the wilderness" (v. 8) hears our plea and answers our payers! He removes from us our obsession with alcohol or drugs and sets us on a new path. This path of sobriety— God's path—brings us ever more hope, freedom, and joy.

The God of Psalm 29 is the God of miracles, the Higher Power who has the strength to save us from death and destruction. Let us stand alongside his children in the temple and shout, "Glory!"

Glory be to you, oh God, who causes the mountains to tremble and saves us from our long suffering! Please use your mighty power to keep us sober today.

Psalm 30

You have turned my mourning into dancing;
    you have taken off my sackcloth
    and clothed me with joy,
so that my soul may praise you and not be silent.
    O LORD my God, I will give thanks to you forever.
                              (vv. 11–12)

I never tire of reading psalms of praise like this one. Psalm 30 tells a before-and-after tale of someone who thought he had it all under control, someone who said, "I shall never be moved." Because of his pride, however, he wrecked his life and came near the "Pit" of death. In his fear and despair, he cried out to God and was saved.

It seems to me that many of the psalms resemble the personal stories we read in the Big Book of Alcoholics Anonymous or hear at a twelve-step meeting. In just a few lines, the author of Psalm 30 tells us what he used to be like, what happened and what his life is like now. Reading this psalm one month into sobriety gave me a great feeling of hope and reassurance. Indeed, the entire history of the world's spirituality is full of stories of people who sometimes did terrible things as they rejected the will of a Higher Power for their lives. People like us. But it is also full of stories of redemption. God never gave up on them, and God won't give up on us.

The psalmist is filled with joy and gratitude because God turned his "mourning into dancing." He cannot help but praise God and not be silent. May we follow his example! When we share with others how the God of our understanding saved us from the hell of our own making, we shine a light in the darkness, helping those still suffering to find a Higher Power and begin their own journeys of recovery.

God, give us the courage to share our experience, hope, and joy with others that they might find your saving grace. Please keep us sober today.

Psalm 31

But I trust in you, O LORD;
   I say, "You are my God."
. . . .
Let your face shine upon your servant;
   save me in your steadfast love.
(vv. 14, 16)

This psalm includes a poetic description of what it can feel like when we hit bottom. In verses 9–12, we read a summary of what life had become for most of us as we neared the end of our nightmares: grief, sorrow, misery, scorn, dread, brokenness. Many of us had become like the psalmist, who was "a horror to his neighbors" and had "passed out of mind like one who is dead" (vv. 11, 12).

We can feel terribly alone at the bottom, and God can seem so far away that he cannot possibly care about us. But just as God heard the pleas of the psalmist in his darkest hour, he will hear our cries for help.

As we learn to trust in the God of our understanding and turn our will and our lives over to God's care, we will find we never again have to be alone. Even in sobriety, life will give us our share of trouble and heartache. But our Higher Power will always provide us a place of refuge from the storm. God's steadfast love never waivers and is always on offer to us. It is a marvelous gift, freely given. All we have to do is accept it.

God, you are our rock and refuge! Help us to trust in your steadfast love, which gives us the courage to face whatever life brings our way. Please keep us sober today.

Psalm 32

> Happy are those whose transgression is forgiven,
>   whose sin is covered.
> Happy are those to whom the Lord imputes no iniquity,
>   and in whose spirit there is no deceit.
>
> (vv. 1–2)

Many things in my life began to improve as I moved further along in my journey of recovery. As the fog began to lift, I could see much more clearly. While this was a positive change, it could also be painful, as my past misdeeds came into sharper focus.

Fortunately for us, the God revealed in the Psalms will forgive even our worst behavior. He requires only two things from us, which Psalm 32 reveals. The psalmist realizes that the weight of his transgressions was sapping his strength and holding him down, causing his "groaning all day long" (vv. 3–4). When he finally got honest with God and confessed his wrongdoing, he received God's full forgiveness and was free from the burdens of the past.

Out of gratitude for his liberation, his trust in God grew as he strove to listen to God's teachings and follow a better way of living. This is how we are transformed by steps four through nine of twelve-step recovery programs. We make an honest accounting of our past and confess our wrongdoing (steps four and five), ask God to remove the defects of character that caused our bad behavior (steps six and seven), and set right our past wrongs as best we can (steps eight and nine). We then are ready to follow God's will and way for our lives through steps ten, eleven, and twelve, keeping us surrounded by God's steadfast love and making us "shout for joy!" (vv. 10–11).

God, we seek your forgiveness for our transgressions. Wash us clean in your love and help us to follow your way for living. Please keep us sober today.

Psalm 33

Truly the eye of the LORD is on those who fear him,
    on those who hope in his steadfast love,
to deliver their soul from death,
    and to keep them alive in famine.

(vv. 18–19)

We learn some important truths as we begin a program of recovery, and our education begins with the question of power. We learn that in our addiction we face a powerful enemy. We learn that human power alone is not enough to defeat this enemy. If the story ended there, we would find ourselves in a truly hopeless situation, indeed. Fortunately, we learn another important truth: there is One who *does* have the power to save us from our disease if only we seek his help.

Psalm 33 is a hymn to God's power. It tells of a God who brought into being the heavens, the earth and all that is in them merely by speaking. It also sings the song of a God who cares deeply about the fate of all creation, a God whose steadfast love fills the world.

The psalmist also shares an important truth with us about how we can move forward into a life of sobriety. Even the efforts of the strongest and most powerful among us will never be enough on their own to save us. Yet this Higher Power's eye is on each one of us. God will be "our help and shield," saving us even from death, if only we call out and follow God's will and way for our lives. Now, *that* is real power!

All-powerful God, maker of all creation, we turn to you to save us from despair and destruction. Please keep us sober today.

Psalm 34

I sought the LORD, and he answered me,
  and delivered me from all my fears.
Look to him, and be radiant;
  so your faces shall never be ashamed.
This poor soul cried, and was heard by the LORD,
  and was saved from every trouble.

(vv. 4–6)

For most of my life, I was locked in an endless cycle of wanting what I did not have. In most areas of existence—relationships, career, material possessions—I suffered from the "grass is greener" syndrome. If only the "right" person would love me, if only I could land that next promotion or raise, if only I could live in a bigger house, *then* I would be happy. If only that were true!

Sometimes we can fall into the same mental trap in sobriety. If only we could move more quickly through the steps, if only we could tell our story in a more compelling way, if only we could be more forgiving, *then* we would be happy!

Psalm 34 is a reminder to take a moment, look around and notice all the incredible things our Higher Power has already done for us. Is everything in my life perfect? Has all that I lost while drinking been restored? Am I done with the hard work of sobriety? No. And I never will be.

Part of what we learn in recovery, though, is that what God wants for us is often different from—and better than—what we might want for ourselves. As we begin to trust his will and way for our lives, we find we gradually lose those selfish desires and are filled instead with gratitude for the unexpected gifts that God so freely gives us.

God, help us to let go of all our striving and selfish ambition. You give us exactly what we need, exactly when we need it. Please keep us sober today.

Psalm 35

Then my soul shall rejoice in the LORD,
  exulting in his deliverance.
All my bones shall say,
  "O LORD, who is like you?
You deliver the weak
  from those too strong for them,
  the weak and needy from those who despoil them."

(vv. 9–10)

In this prayer, we encounter the fears of a man who feels the world is closing in on him but who also trusts in God's power to deliver him. Psalm 35 reminds us that getting sober doesn't mean we will no longer face trouble and difficulty in life. It does mean, however, that we are learning a much better way to handle the inevitable problems life throws in our path.

Before I got sober, I often felt like life was a me-against-the-world proposition. I clung to my own power and ability to overcome the challenges I faced. Often, my own resources proved inadequate to the task, and I sought escape through drinking. Unfortunately, I could never drink my problems away. In fact, they often multiplied as I hid behind a bottle.

God offers us a better solution. When we, like the psalmist, take our struggles to God and lay them at his feet, he will deliver us. Many times, his path through the storms of life will be one that never would have occurred to us alone. Sometimes he calms the storms, and other times he calms us amid the storms we must endure. All we need is a little faith, a little patience, and a whole lot of Higher Power!

Give us the faith and patience, God, to trust in your power to see us through our troubles. Please keep us sober today.

Psalm 36

How precious is your steadfast love, O God!
   All people may take refuge in the shadow of your wings.
They feast on the abundance of your house,
   and you give them drink from the river of your delights.

(vv. 7–8)

In the opening verses of Psalm 36, the psalmist describes what life is like for those obsessed with themselves instead of being focused on God. It would be nice to think he is writing about someone else, but, in truth, this profile describes me in my drinking days better than I would like to admit.

I used to listen to the wrong inner voices too often, especially when drunk. I would hatch all manner of plots and schemes, either to try to get others to do what I wanted or to cover my own tracks. Too often I failed to do the right thing, choosing to behave instead in ways that little by little crossed one ethical line after another. One more lie here, another compromise there, and eventually I could barely recognize the person I had become.

The good news is that no matter how far into immorality we may have fallen, our Higher Power will restore us to who he created us to be. If we can get honest about ourselves and turn to the God of our understanding for help, his steadfast love will be our salvation. We can take refuge under the shelter of his mighty wings and "drink from the river of [his] delights" (v. 8). That will be the sweetest drink we have ever tasted!

God, thank you for turning us from our old ways. Remake us into the person you created us to be. Please keep us sober today.

Psalm 37

Take delight in the LORD,
    and he will give you the desires of your
    heart.
Commit your way to the LORD;
    trust in him, and he will act.

(vv. 4–5)

In this psalm, we have a lengthy lesson in living a counterintuitive life. As we begin the journey of recovery, learning to live by God's principles often means doing the opposite of what our instincts tell us to do. Indeed, sobriety is full of surprising opposites. By admitting defeat, we are able finally to claim victory. By accepting our weakness, we find new strength. By letting go, we begin to get a grip on life. How is this possible?

Our Higher Power can work miracles in our lives, but we need to give him room to work. When we put ourselves in control and try to run our lives by our own will, we are crowding God out. When we try to be master of our own destinies, we worry and fret over every little detail. We try to bend others to our will and can resort to deceit and manipulation to get our way. We can become frustrated and resentful when things don't fall into place. If we follow this path long enough, it will become too much for us, and eventually we will find ourselves on the verge of a relapse.

The God we encounter in the Psalms doesn't want us to struggle through life this way. God wants us to feel the peace, comfort, and strength that God's protection brings. God wants to free us from the burdens of worry and the shackles of regret. As we align "the desires of [our] heart" with God's will for us, we find it becomes easier to do the opposite of what our disease tells us to do. All we have to do is let go and let God show us the way.

God, help us to get ourselves out of the way and give you room to work in our lives. Please keep us sober today.

Psalm 38

My wounds grow foul and fester
  because of my foolishness;
. . . .
I am utterly spent and crushed;
  I groan because of the tumult of my heart.

                 (vv. 5, 8)

The honesty of this psalm is bracing. Here we have a man who has come face-to-face with the painful truth of his own shortcomings, and he is disgusted by what he sees. He also knows that the only way he can free himself from his past is to lay it all out before God and seek forgiveness.

One of the tried and true sayings of twelve-step recovery programs is that our secrets will kill us. We are haunted by the sometimes hurtful and shameful things we have done while under the influence. If we keep these things locked up inside, they will continue to torment us, driving us ultimately back to our substance of choice as we try to escape.

It is a cycle of dread that will eventually kill us, a cycle the fourth and fifth steps are designed to break. It is crucial that we leave no stone unturned, no secret hiding in the shadowy recesses of our souls if we are truly to break free from their oppressive power over us. We cannot flinch from total honesty when we write our inventories (step four) or admit our wrongs to God, ourselves, and another person (step five).

This is hard, scary work, but the reward is great. I feared a return to the hell of my alcoholic existence more than I feared the truth. I finally accepted that the only way to freedom was the road of rigorous honesty. My Higher Power, my sponsor, and my AA friends walked with me, and their strength carried me through to a broad place of forgiveness, freedom, and new hope.

God, grant us the courage to name the demons of our past that still haunt us, that we may experience the glorious freedom of your forgiveness. Please keep us sober today.

Psalm 39

"And now, O Lord, what do I wait for?
  My hope is in you.
Deliver me from all my transgressions.
Do not make me the scorn of the fool."
(vv. 7–8)

We know that God desires full honesty from us in our admission of wrongdoing. We also see throughout the Psalms honest gratitude and praise for God's boundless love and saving power. In Psalm 39, however, we see another kind of honesty—the psalmist's genuine expression of frustration and impatience with God.

Many of our relationships while we are still in the grips of our disease tend to be characterized by dishonesty. We often lie to hide our drinking and using, cover up our bad behavior, and try to get ourselves off the hook. In recovery, we must come clean and face the truth of our past actions, making amends where we can. Going forward, we know our sobriety depends on healthy relationships built on an honest foundation.

The same is true of a relationship with a Higher Power. It is easy to see God as distant and removed. Some of us might have gained a prior notion of God as an angry, punishing, cosmic disciplinarian who expects perfection. As is the case for many of us, though, the God I have come to know in recovery is a loving Father who is never far from me. He seeks an intimate, personal relationship with me. He wants my full honesty and invites me to share with him all that is on my heart—even the frustration or doubts I feel when I think he is too slow to act or is not giving me the help I think I need. If I can't be honest about such things, then they will stand between us, and my Higher Power doesn't want anything to keep us apart.

God, thank you for listening to our complaints and seeking a genuine, honest relationship with us as the people we truly are. Please keep us sober today.

Psalm 40

I waited patiently for the LORD;
    he inclined to me and heard my cry.
He drew me up from the desolate pit,
    out of the miry bog,
and set my feet upon a rock,
    making my steps secure.

(vv. 1–2)

When we think of what our lives used to be like and the miraculous change that the God of our understanding made in us, like the author of Psalm 40 we are driven by joy and gratitude to tell others of this power and saving grace. God's deliverance is a cause for much celebration!

The psalmist's story, however, doesn't end there, and neither does ours. Life did not magically become easy and free of trials and setbacks once God removed our obsession with alcohol or drugs. I'm reminded of a saying from the world of competitive cycling. If you've ever watched a bike race, you probably have seen the "peloton," the big group of cyclists packed tightly together. One moment the peloton can be moving in graceful unison through the countryside, only to be torn apart by a sudden crash the next, with riders and bikes piled in a bloody heap on the road.

It can be difficult not to panic when calamity strikes. A seasoned rider knows, though, that the key to avoiding the crash and remaining upright is to stay calm and focus on the path through the wreckage. As the saying goes, "There will be chaos. Keep pedaling!"

The same is true in our spiritual life. Even in sobriety, life will throw plenty of chaos in our path. But deliverance is not a one-time thing. If we keep pedaling, God's saving grace will always see us through.

God, help us to trust in your power and keep pedaling, no matter what life throws in our path. Please keep us sober today.

Psalm 41

By this I know that you are pleased with me;
   because my enemy has not triumphed over me.
But you have upheld me because of my integrity,
   and set me in your presence forever.

(vv. 11–12)

When I first came to Alcoholics Anonymous, I knew even less than I thought I knew—about myself, the world, why I drank the way I did, and certainly about the AA program. It was scary to realize I really had no clue. With a little openness and willingness, though, I began to learn.

I had a lot of help. I went to a meeting every day and heard other alcoholics share their stories. I read the Big Book and other recovery materials. I read a psalm and prayed each morning. I got a wonderful sponsor who could answer my questions and help me start working the Twelve Steps. I joined a church where I began to build a stronger relationship with my Higher Power and grow in my faith.

As we begin our journeys of recovery, all these things help, and little by little we begin to understand our disease and how the Twelve Steps can transform our lives. But how do we really know if we are working a good program? How do we know if we are living according to God's will for our lives?

Those can seem like difficult questions to answer, but the author of Psalm 41 suggests it's not all that complicated. In verse 11, the psalmist concludes that his own life provides the answers. He knows that the God of his understanding is pleased with him because his enemy has not triumphed over him. We know that we have done at least something right because today we did not drink or use. Thank you, God!

God, may we work a good program today and recommit ourselves to following your will for our lives. Please keep us sober today.

Psalm 42

Why are you cast down, O my soul,
and why are you disquieted within me?
Hope in God; for I shall again praise him,
my help and my God.

(v. 11)

Many of the psalms offer us spiritual guidance for a journey of recovery, and Psalm 42 reminds us of a problem that can plague us whether we have one month or twenty years of continuous sobriety. All of us have those days when we feel irritable and restless, when things seem not to go our way and our reactions make things worse. We often can be at a loss to understand why our serenity seems to evaporate.

The author of Psalm 42 must have been experiencing something similar. This poem has two parts that both end in a similar refrain, found in verses 5 and 11. In the first half of the refrain, he wonders why his soul is downcast and disquieted within him. He could just as well have asked, "Where has my serenity gone?" In the second part of the refrain, he offers himself—and us—the only lasting solution: "Hope in God."

This answer can at first appear too simple, even trite. But the psalmist's experience, and our own, is all the proof we need. It is hope in God that saved us from the brink of death and destruction. It is hope in God that broke the chains of addiction and gave us new life. It is the same hope to which we turn every day to keep us sober.

God replaced our thirst for alcohol with a deep thirst for God's living water. When our serenity seems to evaporate, this spiritual thirst is rising within us. May we then, more than ever, search out God's cool streams and drink our fill of God's peace.

God, we thirst for you as a deer pants for water. Quench our souls with your everlasting peace. Please keep us sober today.

Psalm 43

O send out your light and your truth;
   let them lead me;
let them bring me to your holy hill
   and to your dwelling.

(v. 3)

For years I wandered around in the dark. As my disease worsened and alcohol became my first and last resort, the darkness kept growing deeper and closing in around me until I could barely see.

In a life filled with darkness, hope can be elusive. Fear begins to take over. Dreams for a better tomorrow are swallowed up in the nightmare of a perpetually worsening existence. In all the stories I've heard and read about fellow addicts "hitting bottom," the specific details vary. Each story, however, shares what best can be described as a descent into hopeless, despairing darkness.

It is difficult to know how dark things had become for the writer of Psalm 43, which is a continuation of the same poem that began in the previous psalm. He expresses a hope in verse 3, though, that any alcoholic or addict can appreciate. He calls out for God to send him his light and truth so that they may lead him. We need perhaps nothing more than the light and truth our Higher Power sends to us in the form of the Twelve-Step program. It holds the power to chase away the darkness and restore our hope. It is the light by which we again can dream of a better life. May we let God's light and truth lead us forward in recovery.

Oh God, send us your light and truth to chase away the darkness of alcoholism and addiction. Please keep us sober today.

Psalm 44

For we sink down to the dust;
  our bodies cling to the ground.
Rise up, come to our help.
  Redeem us for the sake of your steadfast love.
                                        (vv. 25–26)

There are days when everything seems to be going wrong. Some days, we can just shake it off and not let it get to us. On other days, our bad habits creep back in. We can start to feel that old self-pity, and maybe we even mix in some righteous indignation. *Why is this happening to me? Have I not been going to meetings? Have I not been praying daily? Did I not just drive someone to a meeting? Have I not suffered enough?*

The community on whose behalf the author of Psalm 44 speaks seems to feel the same way. They believe they have been obedient to God, and yet God did not save them from defeat. Why?

I have often heard others say at meetings that life, with its ups and downs, still happens after we get sober. The reward of faith and a life of sobriety is not special favor or the avoidance of the difficulties that come with being human. The reward is that no matter what happens, we don't have to drink or use and make it worse.

It is always easier to be grateful and faithful when things are going well. But it's when the going gets tough that we most need God's strength, love, and grace to see us through. Whatever difficulties we face, our Higher Power will walk beside us every step of the way.

God, help us always to turn to you, in good times and bad. May we remember that you will never let us walk alone again. Please keep us sober today.

Psalm 45

I will cause your name to be celebrated in all generations;
therefore the peoples will praise you forever and ever.

(v. 17)

While most of the psalms have a theme that relates readily to recovery, we sometimes encounter a poem with a less obvious connection. Psalm 45 is a song of celebration of the king's wedding. We certainly have much to celebrate in recovery, and nothing is greater than our milestones of sobriety. Indeed, for some of us in recovery, our sobriety anniversary can become more meaningful than our birthday.

When I first came to AA, I didn't much feel like celebrating anything, especially myself. I was reluctant to stand up at meetings and share that I had reached thirty, sixty, or ninety days. In part, it felt like an insignificant achievement compared to others who had gone twenty or thirty years without a drink. I also thought so meager an accomplishment as mine, difficult as it was, paled in comparison to the bad things I had done in the past. Plus, getting sober wasn't something I had done on my own power anyway, so why should I get the credit?

Thankfully, my sponsor set me straight. It wasn't mostly about me, he said, but the other people at the meeting. There could be people in attendance with only a day or two under their belts. When we stand and say we've reached a month or three or six, it could give them the hope they need to stay sober just one more day. What we're really celebrating when we share a milestone in sobriety is not ourselves, but the program of the Twelve Steps and the work of a Higher Power. For without them, we would have no cause for joy.

God, help us to humbly celebrate your miraculous work among us. Please keep us sober today.

Psalm 46

God is our refuge and strength,
  a very present help in trouble.
Therefore we will not fear, though the earth should change,
  though the mountains shake in the heart of the sea.

(vv. 1–2)

As part of the fourth step in the program of Alcoholics Anonymous, we are supposed to make a thorough inventory of our fears. At first, I didn't know what to write down. I didn't think of myself as a fearful person. I took pride in being someone who would keep moving forward when others turned back, a man who would never back down in the face of overwhelming odds, the kind of person who could stay calm in a crisis.

As I continued to think and pray about it, though, I was surprised to discover that fear was a powerful force in my life. I was afraid of not measuring up to others' expectations, afraid of not being loved and accepted, and afraid of letting people down. I lived in constant fear that my lies and secrets would be revealed, and I would be seen as the person I really was instead of the person I pretended to be. I was in a near constant state of anxiety as I struggled to keep it all together and stop life from crashing down around me. As my fear and anxiety grew, so did my drinking. For a time, alcohol helped me to hide from my fears, but eventually it only made them grow.

In Psalm 46, we find a promise—the only one that can help us keep our fears at bay. Many of our fears have their roots in our self-reliance, our old belief that we alone have to hold it all together. But, as the psalmist writes, in God we will find "refuge and strength, a very present help in trouble." With God on our side, we truly have nothing to fear.

God, you are our refuge and strength. We turn our fear over to you. May we find release in your saving power. Please keep us sober today.

Psalm 47

Clap your hands, all you peoples;
    shout to God with loud songs of joy.
For the LORD, the Most High, is awesome,
    a great king over all the earth.

                        (vv. 1–2)

Part of the beauty of the Psalms is their honest embrace of the broad range of human emotion. Many of these poems deal openly with the struggles and disappointments of human existence. We find the prayers of people who are sometimes filled with shame over their failings or are stuck in the grip of fear as evil seems to lurk around every corner.

We also find psalms like Psalm 47 that are awash in the joy of being God's chosen people. As the psalmist contemplates God's infinite love and power, he is moved to sing, shout, and clap his hands in praise. Just as sorrow and pain are natural responses to the many wrongs we may have committed or endured, so is joyful celebration the fitting response to our Higher Power's saving grace and the miracle of sobriety.

It can be easy for us to get stuck in the past. Certainly, an honest accounting of our prior misdeeds and recalling all that we sacrificed on the altar of alcohol and drugs are important to our recovery. We must remember, though, that our story does not end there. God's redeeming love has made us whole, and God's awesome power has set us free. That is cause for singing and shouts of joy!

God, we sing your praise and shout for joy at the miracle of your saving grace in our lives! Please keep us sober today.

Psalm 48

We ponder your steadfast love, O God,
   in the midst of your temple.
Your name, O God, like your praise,
   reaches to the ends of the earth.
Your right hand is filled with victory.

(vv. 9–10)

This psalm celebrates the city of God, the divine dwelling place on earth. It is a place where God's people gather together in worship and praise, feeling a special connection to their Higher Power and to one another. The Psalms provide many examples of personal connection with God outside the confines of the holy city but encounters with God in God's temple receive special attention.

I sometimes look at the meeting places of Alcoholics Anonymous as many versions of God's holy city. To be sure, we hold meetings in many different kinds of rooms. Sometimes the buildings where we meet are humble and poorly furnished, nothing like the massive temple with lavish decoration. But God takes up residence there with us and transforms the shabbiest of meeting rooms into the dwelling of the Most High.

We come together to share our experience, strength, and hope with one another. We tell our stories of how God's power saved us from death and destruction. We learn from one another how to better practice a program of recovery and follow God's will for our lives. At our meetings, our temporary Zion, we encounter the God of our understanding in our fellow alcoholics and addicts, and we find the help we need to stay sober one more day.

God, thank you for giving us the gift of Twelve-Step meetings where we can find your strength, hope, and peace. Please keep us sober today.

Psalm 49

Truly, no ransom avails for one's life,
there is no price one can give to God for it.
(v. 7)

I held two major misconceptions that were powerful drivers of my alcoholism. First, I believed that if I could just get everything in my life to line up the way I wanted it to, then I would be happy and satisfied. Second, I believed I possessed the power myself to make that happen.

Psalm 49 tells us just how foolish this way of thinking is. For a while, I succeeded with many of my plans. I advanced my career, built up personal prestige, had a "model" family and amassed considerable wealth. But like Mick Jagger sings in the famous song, I couldn't "get no satisfaction." I remained empty inside, and no achievement or amount of money could fill in the hole in my soul. So, I drank, but alcohol wouldn't fill it either. Not one to be easily defeated, I kept drinking more and more until I had lost nearly everything I had worked for and cherished.

Nothing I could have done myself, I see now, could have saved me. My own power was inadequate to the task, for only God can fill that hole. I am grateful that I finally came to understand that truth, and now every day is a precious gift. In the God of my understanding, I find the joy and contentment that before seemed so elusive.

Thank you, God, for filling the hole in our souls with your love, joy, and peace. Please keep us sober today.

Psalm 50

"Offer to God a sacrifice of thanksgiving,
  and pay your vows to the Most High.
Call on me in the day of trouble;
  I will deliver you, and you shall glorify me."
(vv. 14–15)

In the recitation of "How It Works" from chapter 5 of the Big Book of Alcoholics Anonymous that we sometimes read as a meeting opens, we learn that we are embarked on a program of spiritual progress, not perfection. Thank God! In the honest reflection I try to do every day as a part of the tenth step, it is abundantly clear to me that I often fall short in my practice of the AA program.

In Psalm 50, we find a call sent out to God's faithful to rededicate themselves to following his will and way for their lives. As the psalmist writes, God does not want our sacrifices or excuses. He cannot be bought off from holding us accountable for our shortcomings. What he seeks instead is our honest confession of our wrongdoing, our gratitude for his saving grace, and renewal of our sincere commitment to doing his work.

In our prayer life, we can seek to do just that. I find that when I begin my prayers with thanksgiving and praise for what my Higher Power has done in my life, admitting the ways I continue to fall short and renewing the commitment to turn my will over to God, I open the door to God's ongoing work. We won't always get things right in recovery, but if we bring honesty, willingness, and faith to our efforts, the God of our understanding will continue to reward us with sobriety, one day at a time.

God, forgive us when we fall short and accept our honest plea for your help as we continue on the journey of recovery. Please keep us sober today.

Psalm 51

The sacrifice acceptable to God is a broken spirit;
a broken and contrite heart, O God, you will not despise.

(v. 17)

Pride is sometimes called the greatest of sins because nothing else does more to separate us from God. St. Bernard of Clairvaux wrote a treatise on the topic way back in the twelfth century that describes the steps of descent into prideful living. It begins with simple curiosity about things that are not our concern and ends in habitual wrongdoing. Pride leads us progressively through stages of contempt, first toward other people and eventually toward God. In the prideful way of living, doing what we ourselves want, whatever the cost, whatever the effect on others, matters more than anything else.

In Psalm 51, pride's opposite—humility—is on display. We read in verse 17 that what God seeks from us is a broken and contrite heart. God does not expect us to be perfect, thankfully. What God does expect when we fall short is honest acknowledgment of our wrongs, heartfelt regret when we hurt others, and a renewed willingness to learn and grow.

Humility, it has been said, involves not thinking less of ourselves, but thinking of ourselves less. In order to achieve the kind of honest contrition described in Psalm 51, we should stop thinking about ourselves at least long enough to consider how our actions might have affected someone else. We don't always like what we see when we do this, but fortunately God stands ready to restore us and continue the long process of removing our shortcomings.

God, grant us the humility to focus more on you and others, and less on ourselves. Please keep us sober today.

Psalm 52

But I am like a green olive tree
    in the house of God.
I trust in the steadfast love of God
    forever and ever.
I will thank you forever,
    because of what you have done.
In the presence of the faithful
    I will proclaim your name, for it is good.

(vv. 8–9)

More often than I'd like, I see my old self in the descriptions of the "wicked" in the pages of the Psalms, and certainly Psalm 52 is no exception. I used to be just like the man in verses 1–4, boasting of the things I achieved through plotting and deceit, loving evil more than good.

As the psalmist predicts, I eventually got my comeuppance. My arrogance and dishonesty made me blind to the truth and resentful when my life began to crumble. Having relied so long on my own power and crowed so loudly about my own accomplishments, I was unwilling to turn to God for help. As I leaned ever more on the bottle to escape reality, my pain turned to anger, and I lashed out at those around me.

Overestimation of our own power gives us a false confidence. When our own will finally proves entirely inadequate to save us and the walls fall in around us, we eventually may find just enough willingness and humility to turn to a Power greater than ourselves for help.

Over time, God will slowly replace our arrogance with a new confidence, not in our own power, but in his. If we stand with God, we can never be shaken.

Mighty God, help us always turn to you and your power, giving you the glory in victory and seeking your consolation in defeat. Please keep us sober today.

Psalm 53

Fools say in their hearts, "There is no God."
They are corrupt, they commit abominable acts;
there is no one who does good.

(v. 1)

I struggled with the question of God's existence for many years. It was more of an intellectual challenge for me than it was a spiritual quest. I wanted to be "right" about God—and prove others wrong—and so I read and thought and talked. All of it ultimately led nowhere, to nothing. Unsatisfied with all my research, I declared the question of God unanswerable and myself an agnostic.

I was exactly the kind of fool of which the psalmist writes in the opening lines of Psalm 53. I arrogantly believed that if I couldn't figure out who God was, then God must not exist. I looked down on believers as being too simple and stupid to reject the myths to which they clung, and I sometimes took pleasure in trying to show them what I saw as the flaws in their naive reasoning.

The conscious arrogance of all this was bad enough, but without fully realizing it, I had committed the even greater sin of pride. By declaring the question of God unanswerable on my own meager intellectual authority, I had in essence claimed the role of God for myself. How foolish, indeed!

Long story short: It didn't work out so well. What we often must learn the hard way is that life goes much better when we stop playing God and acknowledge the existence of a Power greater than ourselves. We might not be able to explain it all, but we'd be foolish not to admit that God's way works while ours does not.

Forgive us, God, for the foolish pride that makes us challenge your power. We can't, you can, and we need to let you. Please keep us sober today.

Psalm 54

Save me, O God, by your name,
    and vindicate me by your might.
Hear my prayer, O God;
    give ear to the words of my mouth.

(vv. 1–2)

This psalm is an ode to God's saving power. It is a power that anyone in recovery should know well, as it is the source of our sobriety. We also know that we have our own small part to play, for even God's awesome power cannot save us if we are not willing.

Certainly, willingness is a necessary condition for being set free from the bondage of addiction. We first have to admit our own powerlessness and then be open to the possibility that the God of our understanding can transform us. The need for willingness, however, doesn't end there. If we are to remain sober today, we must remain willing to follow the suggestions contained in the Twelve Steps and continue to submit ourselves to God's will.

This is not always easy. At times, we must be willing to do unpleasant and difficult things. We must make a thorough inventory of our past misdeeds and honestly admit them to God, ourselves, and another person. We must seek God's help in removing our faults and make amends to those we've harmed. We must sometimes trust that what God provides is what we really need, even when it isn't what we really want.

Willingness is crucial to living a sound, sober life. When we remain willing, our Higher Power can accomplish amazing things!

God, help us remain willing to follow where you lead, so that your power can continue to work in and through us. Please keep us sober today.

Psalm 55

And I say, "O that I had wings like a dove!
  I would fly away and be at rest;
truly, I would flee far away;
  I would lodge in the wilderness;
I would hurry to find a shelter for myself
  from the raging wind and tempest."

(vv. 6–8)

I used to fantasize about running away and disappearing off the end of the earth. Sometimes I imagined being alone in a vast expanse of wilderness, and other times I dreamed of going to a new town or city where no one knew me. I wanted to leave all my troubles behind and start over with a clean slate.

I could never actually do it, though. In part, I felt enough of a sense of responsibility to keep me in place, but I also figured my troubles would somehow catch up with me. So, I stayed in place and tried to disappear in a bottle of scotch as my troubles continued to grow.

The real trouble was me, and I could never hide from myself. As the saying goes, wherever you go, there you are. But Psalm 55 reminds us that God is with us everywhere, in every situation. The psalmist is beset on all sides by threats from enemies he thought were friends, and it drives him to despair.

After laying out his fears to God, he reminds himself—and us—of God's steadfast love and protection. Even when the darkness seems to be closing in and everything seems to be falling apart, God will save us, if only we call on him.

God, you are our refuge, an ever-present help in times of trouble. Please protect us and keep us sober today.

Psalm 56

For you have delivered my soul from death,
   and my feet from falling,
so that I may walk before God
   in the light of life.

(v. 13)

Do I really trust God? If I do not, why not? I sometimes ask myself these questions when I'm having a bad day or going through a rough patch. When I'm feeling stress and anxiety about things going on in my life, chances are I'm holding onto them myself and not trusting in God enough to turn them over to him.

Self-will is a sticky thing. When I first came to the third step in the program of Alcoholics Anonymous and tried to turn my will and life over to God's care, I found that my will tried hard to cling to me. Despite my growing awareness that living by my own will had resulted in so much pain and sorrow, I found control a hard habit to break. But there was the rub—as long as I was trying to control my will myself, I wasn't actually turning it over to God and trusting in him.

Psalm 56 gives us a powerful "if/then" reason to trust God more. In verse 13, the psalmist remembers, "For you have delivered me from death, and my feet from falling, so that I may walk before God in the light of life." *If* God has saved him from death, *then* surely, he should trust God to protect him from his mortal enemies.

The psalmist's conclusion applies equally to us. *If* our Higher Power freed us from the prison of our addiction, *then* surely, he will see us through any difficulty life throws our way. "In God I trust; I am not afraid!"

God, help us trust you enough to turn everything over to you so that we may walk in the light of the life you have in store for us. Please keep us sober today.

Psalm 57

Be merciful to me, O God, be merciful to me,
    for in you my soul takes refuge;
in the shadow of your wings I will take refuge,
    until the destroying storms pass by.
I cry to God Most High,
    to God who fulfills his purpose for me.

(vv. 1–2)

The vision of refuge and shelter has always held a powerful attraction for me. From the time I was a boy, I loved to walk deep into the woods, find a quiet place, and just sit. If I stayed there long enough, it seemed the stillness and peace that surrounded me would slowly seep inside and calm the storms that sometimes raged in my heart and mind.

The problem was, I could never stay put in that place and time. Eventually, I had to get up and walk back out into the world. The serenity I found in the woods would stay with me for a while, but it always faded away.

The author of Psalm 57 writes about God as his refuge, finding shelter in the shadow of God's wings. It's a beautiful image, but where do we go to find God's place of refuge for us? The psalmist gives us a clue when he describes lying "down among lions that greedily devour human prey" in verse 4. Even there, "God will send forth his steadfast love and faithfulness."

How amazing! God's refuge comes to us, if only we seek his protection. At times, it can feel like the temptation to drink or use surrounds us on every side. But God will stretch out his mighty wing over us, and in its shadow, we can find sober refuge today.

O God, you are our refuge! We seek shelter in the shadow of your loving wings. Please keep us sober today.

Psalm 58

People will say, "Surely there is a reward for the righteous;
surely there is a God who judges on earth."

(v. 11)

Psalms of God's judgment and punishment can be difficult to read. When I encounter descriptions of the "wicked" and the evil deeds they do, I often recall the life I led before sobriety and feel a sense of shame and remorse wash over me. If I got what I deserved for the things I did as a drunk, life would be unpleasant indeed.

Certainly, there are some harsh images of justice in Psalm 58, and we are reminded of the costs of living contrary to God's will. On a deeper level, though, the psalm is presenting a contrast between the misery of a world in which people have turned their backs on their Higher Power and the beauty and harmony of life as the creator designed it to be. When we follow other "gods," be they alcohol, drugs, money, sex, or just "self-will run riot" (Big Book, p. 62), we put ourselves on a path that leads ultimately to suffering. It might work out for us in the short run, but eventually we will reap the bitter fruits of our wrongdoing. In a sense, rejecting a life lived on a spiritual basis carries its own punishment and poetic justice, as we sow the seeds of our own doom.

But God created us for something better: the abundant life, true freedom, deep joy, and unconditional love that comes through fellowship with him. God stands ready to welcome us back into his loving arms, offering us forgiveness and the strength we need to live according to his will, if only we admit our wrongs and submit ourselves to him.

God, forgive us for putting other gods before you. Help us to live into the life you created us to have. Please keep us sober today.

Psalm 59

O my strength, I will sing praises to you,
   for you, O God, are my fortress,
   the God who shows me steadfast love.
                  (v. 17)

This psalm is largely a plea for God to rescue the community from its enemies. Toward the end, the psalmist identifies two important attributes of his Higher Power that make God the perfect refuge in times of trouble—power and love.

As we begin our journey of recovery, we must come to terms with our own powerlessness. Despite our own best efforts, we could not defeat our disease. We needed a Higher Power stronger than us to get and stay sober. If God did not have the power to remove our obsession with alcohol or drugs, he would not be the refuge we need to protect us from our own enemy.

In verse 17, though, the writer of Psalm 59 praises God not only for being our "fortress," but also for being the one who "shows me steadfast love." This love is the second attribute that makes God our perfect refuge. It is the source from which spring God's mercy and forgiveness, his comfort and consolation, and the guidance we need to live a better life. Protection without love would leave us feeling empty and unfulfilled. Love without protection would leave us feeling vulnerable and weak. But our Higher Power provides both. He is our perfect refuge.

God, you are the perfect refuge, and we are grateful for both your love and your protection. Please keep us sober today.

Psalm 60

O grant us help against the foe,
  for human help is worthless.
With God we shall do valiantly;
  it is he who will tread down our foes.
(vv. 11–12)

As verse 11 reads, "human help is worthless." This assertion recalls the words from chapter 5 of the Big Book of Alcoholics Anonymous that "probably no human power could have relieved our alcoholism" (p. 60). Countless stories confirm for us this basic truth: There is no victory without God.

That is not to say there is no role for humans to play. The God of the Psalms often chooses people as the instrument through which to accomplish God's will. If we are to be of service to others and allow a Higher Power to act through us, then we must be humbly obedient. When we make God's pursuits our own, amazing things become possible.

I sometimes marvel at how the AA fellowship has continued to thrive over so many years without professional leadership, great financial resources, or much in the way of publicity. Many of the most successful nonprofit groups have massive structures of organization and hierarchy. AA, on the other hand, has remained simple and free of bureaucracy. Yet, it has continued to grow, adapting to vast changes in society while remaining true to its core purpose, and serving as the inspiration for other twelve-step recovery programs.

How is this possible? I believe it is the work of a Higher Power. Just as God has done for each recovering alcoholic and addict what we could not do for ourselves, God has sustained our fellowship in a way that human power alone could never achieve. Our shared commitment to following God's will helps keep each one of us sober so that we might welcome those who are still suffering into our midst.

Thank you, God, for the gift of our recovery fellowships. May we keep our focus always on your will for us. Please keep us sober today.

Psalm 61

Hear my cry, O God;
　　listen to my prayer.
From the end of the earth I call to you,
　　when my heart is faint.
Lead me to the rock
　　that is higher than I.

(vv. 1–2)

We encounter in Psalm 61 the prayer of one who feels alone and distant, calling out to God from the end of the earth. He asks for God's refuge and shelter, longing to live out his days surrounded by God's steadfast love.

When I first got sober, I had very little going on in my life. I was estranged from my family, had very few remaining friends, and had lost my job. My days consisted mostly of going to meetings, reading books about recovery and spirituality, and praying. It was a protected isolation not unlike the experience others have shared with me about their time in residential treatment facilities.

As we gradually begin to reengage with the world and move out of the recovery cocoon we sometimes build for ourselves, it can be scary. I remember preparing to take a trip out of town for a possible job opportunity not long after I got sober, and I was afraid. Business trips had always been drinking trips, and I wished I could stay hidden under the shelter of God's wings.

I learned something important on that trip: God is a shelter that travels! I took my Big Book and the Psalms along, found a meeting to attend in the city I was visiting, and prayed often. I didn't drink. While I felt I was going out to the end of the earth, my Higher Power went with me. Wherever we go, God will go with us and keep us sober.

God, your love and power will follow us, even to the end of the earth. May we always seek refuge in you. Please keep us sober today.

Psalm 62

Put no confidence in extortion,
  and set no vain hopes on robbery;
    if riches increase, do not set your heart on them.
Once God has spoken;
  twice have I heard this:
that power belongs to God,
  and steadfast love belongs to you, O Lord.

(vv. 10–12a)

In twelve-step recovery programs, we celebrate the ninth-step promises, a vision of the new life that awaits us in sobriety. Early in our journey of recovery, the promises give us the hope and encouragement to "keep coming back." As they begin coming true in our lives, we are filled with gratitude for what God has done for us.

As our lives begin to improve, however, we can be tempted to shift our focus away from the God of our understanding and toward the incredible gifts we receive through sober living. Psalm 62 reminds us that God alone is our salvation, and it warns us not to allow these gifts to become more important than the giver. "If riches increase," reads verse 10, "do not set your heart on them."

At times, I have seen myself grow overly attentive to the fruits of my recovery rather than the tree that bears them. As recovery advances, we see relationships restored, and opportunities and responsibilities renewed. It is easy to become caught up in these things and forget that they cannot be our primary focus. We didn't earn God's saving grace, nor can we ever, through our own power, be worthy of the gifts we receive. God and sobriety must always come first. Otherwise, we stand to lose everything else.

God, thank you for the increasing abundance you have given us. May we always remember that it all comes from you. Please keep us sober today.

Psalm 63

O God, you are my God, I seek you,
  my soul thirsts for you;
my flesh faints for you,
  as in a dry and weary land where there is no water.

(v. 1)

We alcoholics know what it is like to be thirsty. Our thirst for alcohol grew to the point that it could not be quenched. If we weren't drinking, we were thinking about it. If we were drinking, we were thinking about drinking more. Our thirst became a constant mental obsession that dominated our lives.

When God frees us from this obsession, it is an amazing thing. Over time, we think less and less about alcohol, and when the thought of a drink enters our minds, it leads to a feeling of revulsion at the destruction it would surely trigger.

This transformation in our thinking is miraculous. It is not, however, a cure. We will always be alcoholics, and, as such, God knows that we will always have a mind prone to obsession. Once we are free of our bondage to alcohol, we run the risk of kindling a new obsession with something else.

For this reason, the work of our Higher Power doesn't end with liberation from drinking. If we remain committed to deepening and strengthening our conscious contact with God as we understand him, he will gradually give us the best kind of obsession: thirst for God "as in a dry and weary land where there is no water" (v. 1). This is a thirst that God will be ever willing to quench with his love and abundance.

We thirst for you, God. Pour out your living water on us. Please keep us sober today.

Psalm 64

Hear my voice, O God, in my complaint;
   preserve my life from the dread enemy.
Hide me from the secret plots of the wicked,
   from the scheming of evildoers.

(vv. 1–2)

In Psalm 64, the power of words is on display. In this case it is evildoers who use their words to conspire together to do harm to others. They are ultimately thwarted in their plots as God turns their words against them.

Human language is an amazing thing. As a child, I learned the old rhyme, "Sticks and stones may break my bones, but words will never hurt me." If only that were true! Many times, the words of others have hurt me, and often my own words have injured them. Our speech can be forceful, lifting up those around us or dragging them down.

A word spoken in kindness can be a great gift to someone in need. I received such a gift at an AA meeting one day. I was dealing with the pain of a traumatic experience that someone I love dearly had endured. It was the sort of pain that would have driven me to drink heavily in the past. Rather than keep my feelings bottled up, I shared them with the group when it was my turn to speak. As the discussion moved on around the room, a woman seated next to me handed me a note. It read, "Take it from a victim, the most important thing you can do to help the person you love is stay sober."

In this kind gesture, she told me exactly what I needed to hear at that moment. Her words gave me comfort and strength and helped me stay sober that day. God gave us the power of language to build each other up. How am I using this power?

God, may we use the power of our words to share your loving-kindness with those around us. Please keep us sober today.

Psalm 65

Happy are those whom you choose and bring near
  to live in your courts.
We shall be satisfied with the goodness of your house,
  your holy temple.
By awesome deeds you answer us with deliverance,
  O God of our salvation;
you are the hope of all the ends of the earth
  and of the farthest seas.

(vv. 4–5)

Celebration and praise of God's might and goodness is the theme of Psalm 65. God's awesome deeds that order all creation and save his people are cause for joy and praise. In verse 4, the psalmist writes, "Happy are those whom you choose and bring near to live in your courts." To be chosen by God is an incredible gift—and it can be difficult to understand. In my former life, I sometimes asked, "Why me?" out of a sense of self-pity. Now, in sobriety, I sometimes ask the same question because I feel unworthy of God's rescue when others still suffer.

One way to answer this question is to acknowledge that our Higher Power has a plan for us. When we pledge to follow God's will and not our own, we are offering to be of service to God. There is nothing we can do on our own that can ever make us deserving of God's love, forgiveness, and saving grace. But there is much we can do to honor God's "choosing" of us.

That is what serving others is all about. By freeing us from the slavery of addiction, our Higher Power has given us the chance to be of use in this world. There is no stronger expression of thanks and praise we can offer than by doing the work of helping other alcoholics and addicts and caring for those who still suffer.

Thank you, God, for choosing us as your own. Grant us the strength and courage to use the freedom you gave us to serve others. Please keep us sober today.

Psalm 66

[Y]ou let people ride over our heads;
  we went through fire and through water;
yet you have brought us out to a spacious place.
I will come into your house with burnt offerings;
  I will pay you my vows,
those that my lips uttered
  and my mouth promised when I was in trouble.

(vv. 12–14)

There may have been times in our lives when we tried to bargain with God. Maybe we were sick after a binge and promised we would cut back our imbibing if God would relieve a hangover. Perhaps we swore to be a better person if only God would get us out of a jam.

The problem with prayers like this—besides the fact that we seldom can hold up our end of the bargain—is twofold. First, by presuming that we can negotiate with God, we elevate ourselves to God's level. Talk about delusions of grandeur! Second, such prayers are entirely driven by self-will. We are still trying to shape the world to our liking and attempting to enlist God in our service.

This way of thinking and praying gets our relationship with God totally backward, but Psalm 66 shows how to turn it around the right way. The psalmist's praise of God and sacrifices to him are a *response* to God's love and power. Having witnessed God's saving grace, the writer cannot help but acknowledge his Higher Power's greatness and tell the whole world about it.

There is a deal on offer, but God is the one setting the terms, not us. If we are willing to follow God's will and way for our lives, then God will relieve our burdens and bring "us out into a spacious place" (v. 12). That's a deal that should have us shouting for joy!

All-powerful God, we are thankful you are the one calling the shots. Give us the strength and humility to hold up our end of the bargain. Please keep us sober today.

Psalm 67

May God be gracious to us and bless us
  and make his face to shine upon us,
that your way may be known upon earth,
  your saving power among all nations.
Let the peoples praise you, O God;
  let all the peoples praise you.

(vv. 1–3)

In recovery, we can get real encouragement when someone tells us they have noticed how much we have changed for the better. Sometimes their comments come in the form of a compliment for what they think we have achieved in sobriety. Of course, this feat of radical transformation is God's work, not ours.

Conversations of this nature are a good reminder, both of how far the God of our own understanding has brought us and that none if it could have happened through our own power. Psalm 67 is just such a reminder, too. It tells us of how richly God has blessed his people. In one refrain appearing in verses 3 and 5, it also emphasizes the appropriate response: "Let the peoples praise you, O God; let all the peoples praise you."

This is not the way of the world. In professional sports these days, a common form of celebration after a good play is an athlete beating his own chest. More times than not, the successful play was the culmination of the collective effort of multiple teammates. But the chest-beating seems to send a different message: "Look at *me*! Look what *I* just did!"

There is no room for chest-beating in sobriety, for this miracle of new life is not of our making. Let us instead take a knee, bow our heads, and point heavenward. To God be all glory, honor, and praise, for "God, our God, has blessed us" (verse 6).

God, may you continue to bless us, and may we always praise you, and you alone. Please keep us sober today.

Psalm 68

Ascribe power to God,
   whose majesty is over Israel;
   and whose power is in the skies.
Awesome is God in his sanctuary,
   the God of Israel;
   he gives power and strength to his people.
                                    (vv. 34–35)

In Psalm 68, we find a litany of victories God has won for his people. We read of God's power over many kinds of threats encountered by the Israelites, from the forces of nature to the armies of enemy nations. In response, they form a great procession into God's sanctuary, singing his praises and praying for his continued protection.

The scenes evoke for me a collage of the many AA meetings I have attended. There I have heard countless stories of the victories God has won on behalf of recovering alcoholics, his people. Our stories recount how a Higher Power came into our lives, breaking the chains of addiction, righting past wrongs, healing broken relationships, and restoring what had been lost.

Like the ancient Israelites, we alcoholics and addicts were undeserving of this salvation. We were too often examples of self-will run riot, putting our substance of choice first and everything else second. But in God's infinite mercy, he heard us when we cried out for help and saved us from utter destruction.

So, let us always come together to tell the stories of God's awesome power and steadfast love. Let us have faith in the strength of this Higher Power to keep us sober. Let us shout together the final words of Psalm 68, "Awesome is God in his sanctuary . . . he gives power and strength to his people. Blessed be God!"

God, whose mighty power has won for us victory over addiction, we sing your praises! Please keep us sober today.

Psalm 69

But as for me, my prayer is to you, O Lord.
　At an acceptable time, O God,
　　in the abundance of your steadfast love, answer me.
With your faithful help rescue me
　from sinking in the mire;
let me be delivered from my enemies
　and from the deep waters.

(vv. 13–14)

When we say the Serenity Prayer, we are asking God to grant us the ability to accept peacefully those things over which we have no control. Acceptance is not the same as denying the existence of difficulties. The psalmist is beset on all sides by enemies. He does not ignore what is dragging him down, but instead takes the first step toward acceptance by taking his troubles to his God in prayer. He then takes another step forward by acknowledging that he is powerless to control the outcome. Perhaps he has learned the hard way that no matter what he does, he cannot force his tormentors to back down. He takes the final step toward acceptance by turning control over to his Higher Power and asking for deliverance.

Interestingly, the psalmist moves naturally toward the next part of the Serenity Prayer by focusing on what he *can* control: his grateful response to God's faithfulness. He writes in verse 30, "I will praise the name of God with a song; I will magnify him with thanksgiving." Sometimes, like the psalmist, honestly naming to God the troubles we face can help us to realize what lies beyond our control and turn it over to him. That simple, though sometimes difficult, act often leads to the serenity we need to accept what we cannot change and the faith to entrust it to God's care.

God, we come to you with the things that trouble us. Grant us the peace we need to turn control over to you. Please keep us sober today.

Psalm 70

Let all who seek you
    rejoice and be glad in you.
Let those who love your salvation
    say evermore, "God is great!"
But I am poor and needy;
    hasten to me, O God!
You are my help and my deliverer;
    O Lord, do not delay!

(vv. 4–5)

We find in Psalm 70 an urgent plea for God's help. In the opening and closing verses, the psalmist urges God to be hasty in sending out his saving power. The psalm closes with a rather emphatic, "O Lord, do not delay!"

Patience can sometimes be elusive. The busy lives we lead can cultivate in us a constant sense of urgency. We have time pressures on the job and even in our free time. We struggle to fit it all in, feeling like every aspect of our lives is on the clock.

All this time pressure can make it difficult to stay in the moment. I often find my mind racing ahead to what's next instead of savoring what's now. This hurried way of thinking and being can be a source of anxiety. The more focused on tomorrow we become, the more likely we are to deceive ourselves into thinking we can control what happens. In truth, we cannot. All we usually end up doing is cheating ourselves out of our serenity today.

God is eternal. He has always existed and will go on existing forever. All time for God is now. When I find myself getting impatient with God, it is because I am operating on my time, not his. When I let go of my worry about tomorrow, I find God right here beside me today.

God of perfect timing, help us to let go of our worries about what comes next and dwell with you in the beauty of the present. Please keep us sober today.

Psalm 71

You who have done great things,
   O God, who is like you?
You who have made me see many troubles and calamities
   will revive me again;
from the depths of the earth
   you will bring me up again.

(vv. 19b-20)

The voice of experience speaks through Psalm 71. Likely written by an old man, its words describe the ups and downs we all must face in life. The psalmist praises God as his teacher, refuge, and savior, while also admitting that he has endured—and continues to face—his share of difficulties.

It seems that this man has learned something as he approaches life's twilight—faith. In verse 20, he writes, "You who have made me see many troubles and calamities will revive me again." It seems he has developed something best described as "spiritual muscle memory." As he deals with current problems, he looks to his past and recalls that God always provided protection and guidance to see him through. This reminder of God's steadfast love gives him the faith to realize that his Higher Power will again be his rock and refuge, now and for the rest of his days. It also moves him to rejoice and share with others the story of God's saving power in his life.

Early in sobriety, as we are just beginning to build our spiritual muscle memory, the stories we hear from others about how God has rescued them can help shore up our strength. We can draw on the experience of others when we're afraid and uncertain. And over time, as we build a relationship with a God of our understanding and exercise our spiritual muscles, we will soon find we have our own stories to tell.

God, open our ears to hear the stories of your saving grace and build the spiritual muscle memory to trust in you to deliver us from trouble. Please keep us sober today.

Psalm 72

For he delivers the needy when they call,
    the poor and those who have no helper.
He has pity on the weak and the needy,
    and saves the lives of the needy.

                (vv. 12–13)

The coronation of the king of Israel was the likely setting for Psalm 72. It is compelling evidence that the God of the Psalms is intent on turning the worldly, human way of thinking and acting on its head. Here the prayer for the king stresses his role as champion, on God's behalf, for the poor, the needy, and the oppressed. He is to provide for God's people and seek justice in the land. In other words, the king, the most powerful person in the land, is supposed to be a servant, doing God's work by caring for others. For all of us, there is no more important work than service to those around us. Indeed, this is the ultimate aim to which twelve-step recovery programs lead us.

Most of the Twelve Steps are about fixing what is wrong with us that led us to complete reliance on alcohol and drugs. We first learn to trust God (1–3), and then we clean house through an honest accounting of our own lives (4–5) and by inviting God to transform us (6–7) and restore our relationships (8–9). We then move forward with life on a new basis (10–11), but to what end? So that we may live free from dependence on alcohol and drugs, yes, but also that we may finally be of some service to God and others. As the twelfth step tells us, our transformation culminates in our commitment to "carry this message to other alcoholics, and practice these principles in all our affairs" (*Alcoholics Anonymous*, p. 60).

God, accept us as your humble servants. Continue your work in us that we may be of use to you by loving others. Please keep us sober today.

Psalm 73

My flesh and my heart may fail,
  but God is the strength of my heart and my portion forever.
  (v. 26)

What do we truly desire? Are our attention and energy focused on the right things? The writer of Psalm 73 shares his own answers to these questions, describing an important change he experienced that likely resonates with many of us.

In verse 3, he tells us that he "was envious of the arrogant" and jealous of their "prosperity." He describes how perfect their lives once seemed, free from pain and struggle, full of wealth, health, and power. He resented their material comfort and social status, while he struggled through life despite being obedient to his Higher Power.

Then the psalmist shares an important truth that God revealed to him: Ultimately, those who seek after wealth, power, and status in the world's eyes will "fall to ruin" (verse 18). I'm reminded of a line from a Kansas song, "Dust in the Wind": "All your money won't another minute buy." The psalmist concludes that all his longing was "stupid and ignorant," leading only to an embittered soul (verses 21–22).

He decides to keep his desire set on God, and his attention and energy focused on internal rather than external riches. Those things we receive from God endure forever. Following his will and way is the only path to lasting joy and peace. It is the only path to lasting sobriety. What do we truly desire?

God, help us turn away from chasing that which does not last and turn instead toward the enduring love and abundance you offer. Please keep us sober today.

Psalm 74

Have regard for your covenant,
   for the dark places of the land are full of the haunts of violence.
Do not let the downtrodden be put to shame;
   let the poor and needy praise your name.

(vv. 20–21)

The author of Psalm 74 is pleading with God to deliver the community. They have suffered at the hands of the enemy, and the psalmist urges his Higher Power to act swiftly to bring victory to his people.

When I read in verse 8 how the enemy has "burned all the meeting places of God in the land," I am reminded of the endless assault of our enemies, alcohol and drugs. There is likely not a single recovery meeting place in the world that has escaped the fires of relapse. It is painful to watch our brothers and sisters in sobriety "go back out" into the clutches of addiction. It isn't uncommon for the newcomer to experience a back-and-forth struggle before achieving more enduring sobriety, but relapse can strike anyone, anytime. Sometimes a return to drinking or using can be brief, but other times the enemy claims ultimate victory over one of our fellowship.

Like the psalmist, we call out to the God of our understanding to intervene and restore us. We, too, can become impatient for him to act. But the psalmist doesn't lose faith, and neither can we. Psalm 74 recalls for the community the stories of the great victories God has won for the faithful in the past, just as we share our stories of God's miraculous power in our own lives. From this remembering together, we draw strength together to stay sober one more day.

God, let us take courage and strength from our collective memory of your power among us. Give us enduring faith that you will save us again. Please keep us sober today.

Psalm 75

For not from the east or from the west
   and not from the wilderness comes lifting up;
but it is God who executes judgment,
   putting down one and lifting up another.

(vv. 6–7)

We are conditioned to think of ourselves—human beings—as the primary agents of all that happens in the world. We strive for success and seek to avoid failure, taking the credit and apportioning the blame as we see fit.

Who, though, gets the credit for our sobriety? As we work the steps, we go through an incredible transformation that usually is clearly noticeable to those around us. Speaking from their bias toward human agency in human affairs, these people tend to congratulate us, giving us the credit for this great achievement. This praise can fill us with pride, tempting us to take the credit.

Psalm 75 reminds us in verses 3–5 to stay in our own lane. God is the one with all power, the one who holds the pillars of the earth steady when it totters (v. 3). God is the one who freed us from the prison of addiction and keeps us sober. God's victory is not ours to claim.

The instruction from God is clear in verse 4: "Do not boast; . . . Do not lift up your own horn" (a symbol of pride and arrogance). If we accept the praise for our recovery, then we are taking the first step toward taking back the power over our own lives. That praise and power belong to our Higher Power alone.

God, you have won the victory over addiction, and we give you the credit. Thank you for setting us free! Please keep us sober today.

Psalm 76

Glorious are you, more majestic
than the everlasting mountains.
(v. 4)

We encounter a mighty God in Psalm 76. The poem celebrates his awesome power and the victories he has won over the forces of this world. With military imagery, the psalmist describes how the strong and confident are surprised when God acts to lay them low.

God's limitless power can indeed be unexpected. When I was new to recovery, I read and heard that God had the power to win victory over my alcoholism. It seemed like a bold claim, indeed. How could it be true? I had no idea, but I knew that nothing else I had tried had been successful. Desperate as I was, I decided not to think too much about it and just do what was suggested to the best of my ability.

So, I went to meetings, got a sponsor, and worked the steps. I stayed sober one day at a time, and gradually my sanity returned. My obsession with alcohol was removed! I came to experience just what the Big Book predicted: "We will see that our new attitude toward liquor has been given to us without any thought or effort on our part. It just comes. That is the miracle of it" (p. 85).

This victory over alcohol, as great as any on the field of battle, comes from a Higher Power working in our lives. Let us "make vows to the LORD [our] God and perform them; let all who are around him bring gifts to the one who is awesome" (v. 11).

Awesome God, thank you for the surprising victory you repeatedly win over alcohol. Please keep us sober today.

Psalm 77

I cry aloud to God,
  aloud to God, that he may hear me.
In the day of my trouble I seek the Lord;
  in the night my hand is stretched out without wearying;
  my soul refuses to be comforted.

(vv. 1–2)

Serenity can at times be elusive, as it seems to be for the writer of Psalm 77. Why is this so? In the midst of inner turmoil, is our Higher Power far off, ignoring us? Or are we just sticking our heads in the sand?

If we're being honest, most of us must admit to having days when our prayers are scattered and unfocused, sidetracked by intervening thoughts and worries. The psalmist seems to be experiencing something similar at the opening of this reading, saying, "my soul refuses to be comforted" (v. 2) and "I am so troubled that I cannot speak" (v. 4).

When I encounter such a state of mind, it is usually because a problem I am confronting is filling my thoughts. I often replay it in my mind over and over, trying to search out a solution. Like the psalmist, I sometimes feel that my Higher Power is far off, as I don't feel the comfort I crave or land on any divinely inspired solution. It can lead to a sense of abandonment and self-pity. "Has God forgotten to be gracious?" (v. 9), I, too, ask myself.

For an alcoholic or addict, the land of self-pity is a bad place to get stuck and can suggest an overly selfish focus. The psalmist shows us how to shift gears and bust through this prayer dead end: "I will call to mind the deeds of the Lord; I will remember your wonders of old" (v. 11). If we turn our attention away from our current troubles and put it back on God and his miraculous deeds, we will find that we quiet down, our faith rises up, and our serenity begins to flow back in.

God, may we be reminded of the great things you have accomplished in our lives. Strengthen our trust that you will help us endure any present difficulty. Please keep us sober today.

Psalm 78

Yet he, being compassionate,
   forgave their iniquity,
   and did not destroy them;
often he restrained his anger,
   and did not stir up all his wrath.
He remembered that they were but flesh,
   a wind that passes and does not come again.

(vv. 38–39)

Psalm 78 almost reads like a moral inventory of the people of Israel. This history of a "stiff-necked" bunch recounts many miraculous acts of God to save the Israelites, who promise fidelity, only to rebel and turn their backs on him. God's abundance never seems to be enough for them. So, they complain and cajole God for more, never being satisfied.

When do I turn to God? In times of trouble, yes. I often seek his care and protection, and it is right to ask for help from my Higher Power. Too frequently in my life, though, I have only turned to God to get me out of a predicament, usually of my own making. I may have begged and pleaded for God to save me from ruin, promising to change my ways if he intervened. Then, like the Israelites in the psalm, I forgot my promise, forgot about God and went back to my old ways.

God is not our get-out-of-jail-free card or a magic lamp we can rub to make our wishes come true. We are called to embrace God's will and way because God wants more for us than a continual cycle of failure, frustration, and misery. To break out of this cycle requires us to set aside our self-seeking and embrace our Higher Power. We must always give God control if we are to receive the sustained reward of a joyous and free life of sobriety.

God, forgive our sometimes stubborn refusal to submit to your will and way. Remove the self-seeking that comes between us and leads to our downfall. Please keep us sober today.

Psalm 79

Help us, O God of our salvation,
    for the glory of your name;
deliver us, and forgive our sins,
    for your name's sake.

(v. 9)

As we read a lengthy plea in Psalm 79 for God to act against enemy nations, we come upon an interesting tip toward the middle of the poem. In verse 9, the psalmist follows his request for deliverance by asking God to "forgive our sins."

In the heat of a crisis, we sometimes feel unfairly maligned by others. It can seem as if we are the innocent victim suffering under unprovoked attacks. The Big Book of Alcoholics Anonymous, however, warns against this reflexive way of seeing the world and ourselves. It too easily can trigger the sort of self-pity that for too long provided fuel for the fire of addiction that consumed us.

Instead, we are supposed to engage in honest examination of our actions to determine our own part in difficulties with others. It seems implicit that the psalmist has done something similar, prompting him to ask for God's forgiveness even though he desires God's help.

Usually, this sort of self-reflection will lead us to a fuller understanding of what is going on in a given situation. When we can better see how we have been part of the problem, we can begin to understand how we can be part of the solution. As it says in the Big Book, "Love and tolerance of others is our code" (p. 84).

God, help us to see our own flaws and seek your forgiveness. May we bring love where there is hate. Please keep us sober today.

Psalm 80

You brought a vine out of Egypt;
   you drove out the nations and planted it.
You cleared the ground for it;
   it took deep root and filled the land.

                            (vv. 8–9)

Often while reading the Big Book, I am amazed at the humble beginnings of the Twelve-Step program and the fellowship it cultivated. It is nothing short of miraculous that God gathered together a small group of suffering alcoholics and inspired them to discover a spiritual path to sobriety, building a fledgling community of mutual support and recovery. Just as amazing is how God has continued to bless the work of all of us in recovery, helping us to grow into a movement that continues to save lives.

Psalm 80 is a community's petition for God to save them. It includes a beautiful remembrance of the miracles that established the Israelites in their homeland. The psalmist writes of God bringing "the vine out of Egypt" and planting it in a new land where it grew and thrived. The vine that is God's people is now threatened and suffering, so again they turn to him for deliverance.

The vine metaphor seems equally fitting for the recovery communities we build. And although the recovery movement has thrived for decades, as if transplanted into rich new soil, we remain under threat, whether from our old enemy alcohol or the scourge of new drug epidemics.

When we face threats to our survival, old and new alike, we must join our voices together in prayer for God's deliverance. It is by God's power that our fellowship took root and grew, and it is our Higher Power alone who will enable us to endure.

God who has transplanted so many lost souls in the new soil of sobriety, cause your rain to fall and your light to shine on us, that we may continue to bear your fruit. Please keep us sober today.

Psalm 81

"I would feed you with the finest of the wheat,
and with honey from the rock I would satisfy you."
(v. 16)

A common refrain of Alcoholics Anonymous is "progress not perfection." In this short phrase from the opening section of chapter 5 of the Big Book, "How It Works," we are reminded that we are on a journey that can never be a straight line. Even the founders of AA readily admitted that they regularly fell short in their efforts to practice the principles they had discovered.

As Psalm 81 reveals, God's chosen people also failed to live according to God's teachings. This poem includes a lengthy section in the voice of God describing their struggles to embrace God's will and way and how they suffered when they strayed. Indeed, shortcomings of the spiritual kind seem to carry their own intrinsic consequences as we fail to live into the fullness of the life our Higher Power wants for us.

But Psalm 81 is also about renewal of the covenant between God and us. We are invited to pick ourselves up, dust ourselves off, and try again. We are engaged in a program of spiritual progress, not perfection. Every new day is a gift from God, a new opportunity to take another step forward in our journey of recovery. How will we use this gift today?

Gracious God, thank you for picking us up when we stumble and setting us back on the path of progress. May we use the gift of this new day to take another step closer to you. Please keep us sober today.

Psalm 82

"Give justice to the weak and the orphan;
 maintain the right of the lowly and the destitute.
Rescue the weak and the needy;
 deliver them from the hand of the wicked."

(vv. 3–4)

The world sometimes seems to be falling apart, and Psalm 82 is a prayer to God to put it back together. It opens with the scene of a divine council in which God steps forth to assert authority over the other "gods" who have failed to provide justice and salvation to the weak and needy.

Other "gods," be they money, sex, alcohol, drugs, or some other force that seeks our allegiance, promise an easy path to happiness. But they are weak and empty idols. They sometimes provide temporary comfort and relief but always leave us feeling hollow and unfulfilled in the long run. They play on our weaknesses and stoke the fires of our selfishness, leaving piles of ruined lives in their wake.

The psalmist's Higher Power has the strength and compassion to end the misery of this world's suffering. He rises up and declares in verse 7 that those false gods that enslave us "shall die like mortals."

But when we turn to the light of the true God and embrace his will and way for our lives, his power will flow into us, and we will witness God's victory over the false gods that have so badly deceived us.

God, you are the One who has all power. Shine your light of truth and justice into this dark world that we may follow your way to hope, freedom, and joy. Please keep us sober today.

Psalm 83

Let them know that you alone,
> whose name is the Lord,
> are the Most High over all the earth.
>> (v. 18)

The author of Psalm 83 has composed a prayer for the deliverance of his community from its enemies. He recalls God's victories as he calls for God's intervention anew, remembering that God's power is always enough.

As people in recovery, we, too, renew the call for our Higher Power to deliver us from our enemy. I find in Psalm 83, as in so many of the psalms, a useful pattern for my own prayers. I often begin to pray by recalling the great victory God won in my life, freeing me from the prison of my addiction. I give thanks for my sobriety and the new life God has given me, blessed with hope, strength, joy, and peace.

This kind of prayerful remembering can reinforce our faith, so that when we ask our Higher Power to keep us sober today and help us with any difficulties we face, we do so from a place of confidence in God's power to deliver us again. Against all odds, the God of our understanding rescued us from addiction. What should we fear? Why would we ever doubt this power?

We also offer our prayers for those who are still sick and suffering, those still in the clutches of their disease. For them we offer the words of verse 18, "Let them know that you alone, whose name is the Lord, are the Most High over all the earth."

Most High God, who vanquished our great foe, please keep us sober today. And may those still sick and suffering find you now.

Psalm 84

How lovely is your dwelling place,
    O Lᴏʀᴅ of hosts!
My soul longs, indeed it faints
    for the courts of the Lᴏʀᴅ;
my heart and my flesh sing for joy
    to the living God.

(vv. 1–2)

There is a cause-and-effect chain in Psalm 84 that is instructive for the development of our spiritual lives. It proceeds from the longing of the soul, through time spent in God's dwelling place, and ends in happiness. In other words, the psalmist deeply desires connection with this Higher Power, the source of his joy, and so he is compelled to seek God out.

To me, this kind of understanding is a mark of spiritual maturity. Early in sobriety, when my relationship with God was in its infancy, I sought to connect to a Higher Power by going to meetings and church out of a sense of obligation. I was afraid of drinking again, and others, who had what I wanted, told me that going to as many meetings as possible would help keep me sober. So, I started going to meetings nearly every day, mainly out of a sense of fear and desperation.

Eventually, my motivations shifted to the point where I was drawn to meetings and church more by the desire for the positive effects—joy, peace, strength—than by fear of the negative. I traded my old cause-effect chain (misery–drinking–more misery) for a new one (love of God–communion with God–happiness and peace). That certainly makes "my heart and my flesh sing for joy" (v. 2).

Thank you, God, for drawing us closer to you where we find what we've always been looking for. Please keep us sober today.

Psalm 85

You forgave the iniquity of your people;
    you pardoned all their sin.
You withdrew all your wrath;
    you turned from your hot anger.

(vv. 2–3)

Forgiveness is vital to our whole project of recovery. As we first get sober, we are eager to be relieved of the burden of guilt we carry. This burden can grow especially heavy after we finally get honest about our past misdeeds in our fourth and fifth steps. We long to be forgiven by God and other people for the wrongs we have done.

We also come to realize that forgiveness is a two-way street. We must let go of our resentments, and we ask God to "forgive us our trespasses as we forgive those who trespass against us." That can be a tough standard to meet, but we soon learn that forgiving others is as much about maintaining our own serenity (and sobriety) as anything else.

Psalm 85 describes what it is like to live in a world where forgiveness reigns. "Steadfast love and faithfulness will meet; righteousness and peace will kiss each other" (v. 10). It is a world full of good things. How much better is such an existence than one dominated by resentment, revenge, and hatred!

Our Higher Power gets the ball rolling by offering forgiveness to us, even though we cannot earn, nor do we deserve, this grace. When we pay it forward by forgiving others, we bring more love into this world and joy and serenity into our own hearts.

God, grant us the loving heart and courage to forgive others as you have forgiven us. Please keep us sober today.

Psalm 86

I give thanks to you, O Lord my God, with my whole heart,
  and I will glorify your name forever.
For great is your steadfast love toward me;
  you have delivered my soul from the depths of Sheol.

(vv. 12–13)

In the list of the ninth-step promises found in the Big Book of Alcoholics Anonymous (p. 84), we are told "we will intuitively know how to handle situations which used to baffle us." In essence, this is a promise that we will be better able to manage the ups and downs of life. This newfound ability is made possible by the transformation that God works within us as we work the steps and is sustained by our commitment to improving our conscious contact with God as we practice the eleventh step day in and day out.

That is exactly what is unfolding in Psalm 86. The psalmist is beset by some difficulty in his life. Rather than holding onto his fear and anxiety, he takes them to his Higher Power in prayer. A closer look at the psalmist's approach can be instructive for us. First, he spends much of his time recalling God's power, love, and grace, thanking God for having delivered him from the depths. The psalmist also asks, "Teach me your way, O LORD, that I may walk in your truth" (v. 11). He spends more time and energy in seeking God's continued transformative work in his life than he does describing his immediate problems.

Indeed, when we prayerfully consider God's power and love for us and ask only for deeper understanding of God's will for our lives and the power to carry it out, the baffling usually becomes much more intuitively manageable. It is as if the answer was inside us all along, but only the God of our understanding could help us find it. That is the power of prayer!

God of steadfast love and awesome power teach us your will and way that we may more intuitively do the next right thing. Please keep us sober today.

Psalm 87

And of Zion it shall be said,
"This one and that one were born in it";
for the Most High himself will establish it.
The Lord records, as he registers the peoples,
"This one was born there."

(vv. 5–6)

In this hymn to Zion—a perfect image of God's city, Jerusalem—important elements of God's character are revealed. Some scholars interpret Psalm 87 as a song of remembering God's dwelling place by those living in exile from their homeland. Others suggest the psalm speaks more symbolically as a call to all God's children to come home to him.

What an amazing thought: We are *all* God's children. We do not belong to God because of our race, gender, ethnicity, or nationality. Not our status, profession, achievements, education, or wealth can qualify us. In fact, nothing that can be done by human power alone will earn us the right to be called a child of God, a citizen of Zion. "The Most High himself will establish it" (v. 5).

I get a chill when I envision my Higher Power, at the moment of my birth, writing my name in the book of God's children, claiming me as God's own. Like many alcoholics and addicts, my journey to Zion has been long and difficult because of the many detours I have taken. Finally, though, I opened my ears to hear my Father's voice calling me home. Thanks to the gift of sobriety, each one of us can rest in God's warm embrace today!

Loving Creator, who wrote our names in your book, thank you for calling us home! May we dwell together with you all the days of our lives. Please keep us sober today.

Psalm 88

O LORD, God of my salvation,
   when, at night, I cry out in your presence,
let my prayer come before you;
   incline your ear to my cry.

                      (vv. 1–2)

"I am desperate." Those words from verse 15 sum up the condition expressed in Psalm 88. We find here the prayer of someone who has given up nearly all hope. The psalmist is so overwhelmed by sorrow and suffering that all he can do is cry out for God's help. There is no expression of hope or faith, only despair.

I know this place. It is exactly where I found myself on my final day of drinking. My life had imploded and lay in ruins all around me. My mind and body were sickened, my relationships broken. Not even alcohol could make me feel better, no matter how much I drank. Most of the time, I didn't even want to go on living. I only wanted the pain to end, but I didn't know how to make it stop. I felt like a lost cause.

And yet, there was just enough of a flicker of life left in me that I thought of God. I was no longer a spiritual person, having turned away from God years before. I had no expectation of divine intervention, but it was my last resort. And so, I prayed the simple prayer of a desperate man, "God, please help me!"

We don't know what happened to the writer of Psalm 88, but I hope he experienced what many of us did—the power and saving grace that only comes from a Higher Power. Since saying that simple prayer, I haven't had to take another drink. God lifted me up out of the hell of my old existence and gave me hope and new life. And God can do for each of us what we could not do for ourselves.

God, we thank you for hearing our cry, saving us from despair and death, and giving us new life. Please keep us sober today.

Psalm 89

Righteousness and justice are the foundation of your throne;
  steadfast love and faithfulness go before you.
Happy are the people who know the festal shout,
  who walk, O LORD, in the light of your countenance.

(vv. 14–15)

Some background is useful for understanding what is going on in Psalm 89. Basically, the psalmist is reminding God of the covenant he made with his people through his chosen king, David. From the author's vantage point, God promised to uphold the king's power and ensure the safety and strength of the nation across successive generations, even if the king and the people strayed from God's will and way.

Likely written after the nation has suffered a major defeat, Psalm 89 suggests that God has not upheld his end of the deal. "You have renounced the covenant with your servant" (v. 39) and "laid his strongholds in ruins" (v. 40), the psalmist accuses. He ends his prayer by imploring God to make good on the promise.

We, too, have been promised a better life in sobriety, but we have not been promised the proverbial rose garden. Even if we work the best program we can and follow God's will as closely as possible, we will still face our share of difficulty and pain. Life, with its good and bad days, still happens in sobriety. So, we might ask along with the psalmist, what's the point?

Simply put, if we keep doing the next right thing and keep to the program for living that our Higher Power has given us, then we don't have to drink or use and make it worse. We don't have to respond to calamity by handing over our serenity, hope, and freedom. We now have the choice to turn to the God of our understanding rather than a mere substance. Which one has the power to sustain us?

God, we choose you! When bad things happen, may your steadfast love comfort us and your power see us through. Please keep us sober today.

Psalm 90

Turn, O LORD! How long?
  Have compassion on your servants!
Satisfy us in the morning with your steadfast love,
  so that we may rejoice and be glad all our days.
                                                    (vv. 13–14)

Time is an important theme in Psalm 90, especially the eternity of God and the mortality of humans. In verses 4 and 5, the psalmist writes that a thousand years for God are like yesterday; God sweeps a millennium away "like a dream, like grass that is renewed in the morning." The days of humans, who are doing well to get seventy or eighty years, in the author's view, "come to an end like a sigh" (v. 9).

This acute awareness of mortality seems to evoke in the psalmist a natural desire for God to grant him more good days than bad. In verse 15, he asks for God to "make us glad as many days as you have afflicted us, and as many days as we have seen evil." It is as if he's saying, "OK, God. I know we messed up, and I know bad behavior has consequences. But life is short, so can we get to the good stuff before it's too late?"

Those of us, like me, who got sober later in life sometimes feel the same way. When we think of the decades of life spent in the grips of our disease, we can become remorseful about lost time and impatient for the better life ahead. The only thing such thoughts achieve, though, is to rob us of today. Yesterday has gone away, tomorrow is promised to no one, but today is a gift from God. May we savor it and use it wisely.

Eternal God, who is and was and ever shall be, help us to dwell in the splendor of this moment that is your gift to us. Please keep us sober today.

Psalm 91

For he will command his angels concerning you
    to guard you in all your ways.
On their hands they will bear you up,
    so that you will not dash your foot against a stone.
                   (vv. 11–12)

When we read the Psalms, we must remember that we are reading prayerful songs that are written in poetic language. Poetry can be challenging for the reader because it does not present us with a factual description to be processed with our rational minds. Rather it is intended to spark an imaginative, emotional response.

Psalm 91 is packed with just such beautiful images designed to help us grasp what it means when we say with the psalmist that God is "my refuge and my fortress; my God, in whom I trust" (v. 2). In the verses that follow, we see pictures emerge that bring to life the truth of God's protection. God will cover us with his wings (v. 4), shield us from violence and terror (vv. 4–5) and save us from disease and destruction (vv. 6–7). Even when we walk where we shouldn't, the fangs of the lion and snake will not harm us (v. 13).

All these illustrations are designed to drive home the point made in God's own words in verses 14–16: God will deliver, protect, rescue, honor, and save those who trust and rely on him. The imagery helps us understand that there is no evil or danger, no matter how great, that can overtake us if we rely on the One who has all power. When our security is in the God of our understanding, then we can, as the Big Book says, "[cease] fighting anything and anyone—even alcohol" (p. 84).

God, you are our refuge and our fortress. What shall we fear?
Please keep us sober today.

Psalm 92

The righteous flourish like the palm tree,
and grow like a cedar in Lebanon.
They are planted in the house of the LORD;
they flourish in the courts of our God.

(vv. 12–13)

We hear the call once again in Psalm 92 to praise God with singing and music. It is specifically for his Higher Power's works that
the psalmist offers his praise, works that display the steadfast love
God has for those who follow his will.

The psalm draws on natural images to demonstrate an important contrast between the "wicked" and the "righteous." The
wicked are described as grass in verses 7–9, springing up and
flourishing quickly before withering and being scattered. The
righteous, in contrast, are like trees with their roots in the "house
of the Lord." Even as they grow old, they continue to "produce
fruit; they are always green and full of sap" (vv. 13–14).

As alcoholics and addicts, we usually sought a shortcut to
relief. We didn't want to wait patiently to sink deep roots and
grow steadily. We wanted to spring up fast like the grass, living
for instant gratification.

In sobriety, we come to embrace the solidity and stability we
find in living one day at a time with the program of the Twelve
Steps. As we sink our roots deeper into recovery's fertile soil, we
find we are less shaken by the winds of life. Each day, our Higher
Power strengthens and nourishes us as we continue to grow
stronger and begin to bear the fruit of a sober life.

*God, may the sap of your will continue to flow through us
that we may bear more of your fruit each day. Please keep us
sober today.*

Psalm 93

The LORD is king, he is robed in majesty;
  the LORD is robed, he is girded with strength.
He has established the world; it shall never be moved;
  your throne is established from of old;
  you are from everlasting.

(vv. 1–2)

The problem of selfishness is of primary concern in twelve-step recovery programs. On page 62 of the Big Book, we are told, "Selfishness—self-centeredness! That, we think, is the root of our troubles." I've also heard people, on the other hand, refer to AA as a selfish program, referring to the program's teaching that if we fail to place maintenance of our sobriety before all else in our lives, we will surely lose it. Yet in Psalm 93, we find a full-throated assertion that God is king, enthroned above all.

What are we to make of these claims, which could seem in conflict on the surface? For me, it comes down to the question of ends or motive. As I go about my day, am I putting myself on the throne, seeking to control people and things to achieve my own selfish advantage? Or am I acknowledging God's rightful place on the throne and seeking to do God's will?

If we start playing god and pursuing our own ends over God's, then we are truly living a selfish existence. Sober living calls us instead to be relentless in our selflessness and always keep our Higher Power on the throne. As it says in verse 4 of our psalm, "majestic on high is the LORD." We must always strive to put God's will before ours.

God, remove from us every impulse to place our own will above yours. You are enthroned over all creation, and you alone are master of our lives. Please keep us sober today.

Psalm 94

When I thought, "My foot is slipping,"
  your steadfast love, O Lord, held me up.
When the cares of my heart are many,
  your consolations cheer my soul.

(vv. 18–19)

After reading the description of the wicked in verses 4–7 of Psalm 94, I am left to wonder: How conscious is their denial of a Higher Power? Do they literally, verbally boast of God's blindness and deafness to their evil deeds, or is it instead their actions alone that reflect their dismissive attitude toward God?

During my drinking days, I continually behaved as if God could not observe the things I thought and did. In my case, it was less an explicit denial that God was paying attention to the pain I was inflicting on myself and others than it was a complete dismissal of the idea of God altogether. By ignoring God entirely, I didn't need to trouble myself with questions of how closely he might be paying attention.

The author of Psalm 94 offers some wisdom. He asks in verse 9, "He who planted the ear, does he not hear? He who formed the eye, does he not see?" These are rhetorical questions, and the psalmist asserts faithfully in the following verses that indeed the God of his understanding hears and sees all.

This truth, however, is a source of strength and joy for those who follow God's teachings. While God watches as his lost children sow the seeds of their own doom, he is equally attentive to the plight of those who follow God's will and way. We can say with the psalmist, "When I thought, 'My foot is slipping,' your steadfast love, O Lord, held me up" (v. 18).

All-seeing, all-knowing God, thank you for caring about every detail of our lives. You give us respite from days of trouble and consolations to cheer our souls. Please keep us sober today.

Psalm 95

In his hand are the depths of the earth;
    the heights of the mountains are his also.
The sea is his, for he made it,
    and the dry land, which his hands have formed.

                          (vv. 4–5)

Psalm 95 introduces a series of psalms of praise that empha-size a core message of the entire collection of prayerful poems: God alone is all-powerful and worthy of our praise. Indeed, this concept of a Higher Power is central to the Abrahamic faiths (Judaism, Christianity, and Islam) and to twelve-step recovery programs. It seems we can never be reminded enough of the ben-efits of fully embracing this truth—and the cost of forgetting it.

A reminder of the cost comes in verses 8 and 9 of Psalm 95. The psalmist recalls for his readers how their ancestors lost faith and put God to the test in the wilderness, demanding that God give them fresh water to drink and food to eat. Despite God hav-ing just freed them from slavery in Egypt and then leading them away from Pharaoh's pursuing armies, the people still could not trust that he would provide for their basic needs. And, so they complained and doubted, even suggesting they might have been better off in captivity.

In our first few months of sobriety, we often feel like we are wandering in a wilderness. We still suffer from the consequences of our addiction, and the future can seem uncertain and scary. We sometimes even wonder whether a return to drinking and using might make us feel better. Gradually, we learn that all we must to do is focus on today, do what is asked of us, and leave tomorrow to our Higher Power.

God who set us free from our bondage to alcohol and drugs, may we trust each day in your power and steadfast love to sustain us. Please keep us sober today.

Psalm 96

O sing to the LORD a new song;
  sing to the LORD, all the earth.
Sing to the LORD, bless his name;
  tell of his salvation from day to day.
                                    (vv. 1–2)

We encounter the first of four closely related psalms of praise in Psalm 96. The opening line, "O sing to the Lord a new song," is repeated in the first verse of Psalm 98, and Psalms 97 and 99 share the same beginning words, "The LORD is king."

Scholars have concluded that, beyond being beautiful hymns of praise, something important in the history of the Jewish people's understanding of right relations with their Higher Power is reflected in these four psalms. In other psalms written at the height of the nation's power under the dynasty that began with King David, we can see a focus on human rulers anointed and chosen by God. In Psalm 96 and the three that follow, which were likely written after the fall of the Davidic monarchy and the nation's defeat, we see acknowledgment of God as the only true Lord and king of the people.

I am reminded again of words from the Big Book that "probably no human power could have relieved our alcoholism" (p. 60). The Jewish people learned a similar hard truth. As they relied ever more on the power of human kings, shifting their allegiance away from God alone, they were severely disappointed, enduring conquest and exile. The good news for them—and us—is that God could and would offer his saving grace, if only he were sought.

God who is to be revered above all else, may we turn not to our own inadequate human solutions, but trust in your saving power alone. Please keep us sober today.

Psalm 97

The LORD is king! Let the earth rejoice;
let the many coastlands be glad!

(v. 1)

As mentioned in the previous entry, Psalm 97 begins with the same opening line, "The LORD is king!" as Psalm 99. Both psalms focus on God's power over all creation, and here it is seen as a cause for rejoicing.

In verses 3–6, images of fire, lightning, mountains, and heavens illustrate the extent of God's dominion over the forces of nature. In verse 7, the psalmist writes of God's superiority over other "gods," which is taken as a reason to be glad and rejoice in verse 8.

When we find references to other "gods" in the Psalms, the original reference was likely to the deities worshiped by other ancient peoples in the region. It is also possible to read this as a reference to anything in our lives that might claim the rightful place of our Higher Power as ruler over all.

While it is unlikely that many of us ever thought consciously of alcohol or drugs as gods, most of us behaved as if they were our higher power. Drinking and using consumed our thoughts and controlled our actions, demanding ever more obedience with a relentless call for complete dominance over our lives.

As the psalmist tells us, though, God has the power to defeat any other force that tries to control us, if only we seek his help. Our Higher Power's victory over these "gods" is definitely cause for rejoicing!

O God, you are the one true king with power over all. We rejoice in your victory over addiction! Please keep us sober today.

Psalm 98

O sing to the LORD a new song,
    for he has done marvelous things.
His right hand and his holy arm
    have gotten him victory.

(v. 1)

As in Psalm 96, "O sing to the LORD a new song" opens Psalm 98. Here the song of praise is prompted by the victory God won for the people of Israel over their enemies, not unlike the victory God has won for us over addiction.

In other psalms, the focus is placed more on the extent and nature of God's power, but in Psalm 98 it is the *effect* of this power that gets the most emphasis. It is one thing to be told God is all-powerful and quite another to witness the tangible difference this power makes in the world of human affairs.

I was skeptical of the claims of Alcoholics Anonymous when I first heard them. It seemed too good to be true that by just working the steps and living my life on a spiritual basis I could be relieved of my obsession with alcohol. Similarly, some of the claims about God's power in the Psalms seemed a bit far-fetched.

For exactly this reason, heeding the call in Psalm 98 to sing praise of God's real-world victories is so important. As others in recovery share their stories of God's victory in their lives, the claims of God's power become more believable. We desperately want what they have, so we begin to do what they did, to the best of our ability.

We sing God's praises due in part to our gratitude for a better life, but we also sing so that others can find hope for their own recovery. Let us join our voices together that those still suffering might find what we have.

Victorious God, we praise you for saving us from the hell of our addiction. May we lift our voices that others can hear and believe. Please keep us sober today.

Psalm 99

The Lᴏʀᴅ is king; let the peoples tremble!
　He sits enthroned upon the cherubim; let the earth quake!
The Lᴏʀᴅ is great in Zion;
　he is exalted over all the peoples.

(vv. 1–2)

The last in our close group of four hymns of praise opens with "The Lᴏʀᴅ is king," as does Psalm 97. In that prior psalm of God's kingship, we read of God's power over the forces of nature and other "gods," a cause for our rejoicing. Here in Psalm 99, the attention is on God's dominion over "all the peoples" (v. 2), a cause for our obedience.

We alcoholics and addicts don't like to be told what to do, and so "obedience" to a Higher Power can be a difficult concept for us. After all, we are taught that the Twelve Steps are "suggestions." Indeed, had they been presented to us as "rules," many of us might have walked right back out the door!

What, though, is the nature of obedience to God? And what should we take from the fact that the Twelve Steps are suggestions? I tend to think about it this way: A parent could tell a child, "I *suggest* you do not touch that burner on the stove; it will burn your hand." The child can then choose to touch the burner and feel pain or follow the suggestion and avoid it.

Obedience means living a life in harmony with God's teachings so that we will avoid causing ourselves more pain. It's not about God punishing us. Living by our own will carries its own intrinsic punishment when we defiantly reach out and touch the burner. Fortunately for us, God is a "forgiving God" (v. 8), ready to welcome us back and soothe our pain when we stray.

God, thank you for giving us a better way to live. Forgive us when our pride leads us to choose our own way over yours. Please keep us sober today.

Psalm 100

Know that the LORD is God.
It is he that made us, and we are his;
we are his people, and the sheep of his pasture.

(v. 3)

We all have obligations in life. We must take care of our children, show up to work, pay our bills, obey laws, and so on. Many of us now in recovery weren't very good at consistently meeting our obligations when we were drinking and using, and we sometimes paid a heavy price. As we get sober, we become better able to do what is required of us in life, although we might not always enjoy it.

Psalm 100 encourages us to think of time spent with God not as an obligation, but as a joy. "Worship the LORD with gladness; come into his presence with singing," it says in verse 2. I don't know about you, but I don't ever remember singing as I paid my bills, and I'm not always glad about getting up early for work! When I pause for a moment on verse 3, though, a very different feeling fills my heart: "Know that the LORD is God. It is he that made us, and we are his; we are his people, and the sheep of his pasture."

What joy this should give us! To be sheep of the Good Shepherd means that we are always under God's care. He watches over us and protects us, leading us to green pastures of abundance and cool, life-giving waters. When we think of God's steadfast love and faithfulness to us, our response of thanks and praise is no obligation. It is a glad privilege!

God, we come to you with a glad heart and thankful spirit. May we always sing praise to you for the miracle you have worked in our lives. Please keep us sober today.

Psalm 101

I will study the way that is blameless.
　　When shall I attain it?
I will walk with integrity of heart
　　within my house;
I will not set before my eyes
　　anything that is base.

(vv. 2–3)

The words of Psalm 101 are spoken in the voice of King David. He lays out his plan for ruling as God's servant leader and gives us what turns out to be a pattern for a good life in recovery.

He begins in verses 1 and 2 by putting God first and admitting he still has a lot to learn. He then commits himself to integrity and turning away from those who choose the wrong path. He says in verse 4 that "Perverseness of heart shall be far from me," and pledges in verse 5 to stand against dishonesty and arrogance. He promises in verse 6 to keep company with others who seek to live by God's will and learn from them, steering clear of those who practice deceit and "utter lies" (v. 7).

King David's words evoke the Four Absolutes of Alcoholics Anonymous, especially honesty and purity. Certainly, living by the Absolutes involves learning a new way to see ourselves and the world. Like David, we must continue humbly to study God's teachings and learn from others. But that knowledge is only useful if we have the determination to put it into practice.

By following the psalmist's example and staying away from those with dishonest and impure motives, we will find that doing the next right thing will come more easily for us. As it says on page 13 of the *Four Absolutes*, "In Purity as in Honesty, the virtue lies in our striving. And like seeking truth, giving our all in its constant pursuit, will make us free even though we may never quite catch up to it."

God, may you continue to teach us your ways as we seek to live a life of honesty and purity. Please keep us sober today.

Psalm 102

Let this be recorded for a generation to come,
    so that a people yet unborn may praise the LORD:
that he looked down from his holy height,
    from heaven the LORD looked at the earth,
to hear the groans of the prisoners,
    to set free those who were doomed to die.

(vv. 18–20)

Had I been able to find the words, I might have prayed like the writer of Psalm 102 the day I finally stopped drinking. I can see my own desperation at the time reflected in the lines of this poem. My body and heart ached (vv. 3–4), I couldn't eat or sleep (vv. 4 and 7), I felt alone and rejected (vv. 7–8) and I could feel my will to live slipping away (v. 11).

This is what it is like when we hit "bottom," that terrible, dark place of despair and loneliness. It is a place without the confidence in a Higher Power the psalmist expresses in verses 12–17. If we turn to God in that moment, we may not even have any expectation of rescue. We might be calling out to God only because we have nothing else left to do.

I have heard others in the recovery fellowship say, "The Twelve Steps were the last thing I tried and the first thing that worked," and so it was for me. As I prayed my own simple, desperate prayer to God and began going to recovery meetings the following day, I was given just a little bit of hope and mustered just enough willingness to keep coming back.

What miracles God can work with a pinch of hope and willingness! As the psalmist writes, "he looked down from his holy height, from heaven the LORD looked at the earth, to hear the groans of the prisoners, to set free those who were doomed to die" (vv. 19–20). As it turns out, the last thing we try often becomes the best thing we could have hoped for.

God, thank you for lifting us out of the pit of despair and making our "bottom" a foundation for a new life. Please keep us sober today.

Psalm 103

Bless the LORD, O my soul,
   and do not forget all his benefits—
who forgives all your iniquity,
   who heals all your diseases,
who redeems your life from the Pit,
   who crowns you with steadfast love and mercy,
who satisfies you with good as long as you live
   so that your youth is renewed like the eagle's.

                       (vv. 2–5)

Imagine yourself in a wide-open field with no trees in sight, the wind swaying the tall grass. You look to the eastern horizon where the sun rose in the morning, and then across the expanse of blue sky to the west where it will set in the evening. How far is it from east to west?

We cannot even measure this limitless distance as the horizon will always recede from us if we try to move toward it. This is how far God removes our transgressions from us when we seek his forgiveness, the psalmist says in verse 12. Earlier in the psalm, he tells us God offers this forgiveness, along with healing, redemption, and love, for a reason: "so that your youth is renewed like an eagle's" (v. 5).

This poetic line evokes the annual process of molting, whereby the great bird of prey sheds old feathers for new. In other words, God's love and forgiveness has a point. He intends to remake us into the people he created us to be. He removes from us completely our misdeeds and mistakes so that we can shed our guilt and remorse, those tattered old feathers that would keep us from soaring.

Bless your name, O God, for your expansive mercy. May we let go of our guilt over past wrongs so that we may love others as you love us. Please keep us sober today.

Psalm 104

You set the earth on its foundations,
so that it shall never be shaken.
You cover it with the deep as with a garment;
the waters stood above the mountains.

(vv. 5–6)

I find great peace in Psalm 104. In many of the psalms, we are reassured that God will comfort and strengthen us in times of trouble. Here we find a very different kind of reassurance. The psalmist uses beautiful descriptions of God's creation to illustrate the magnificent harmony that he intended for the world and everything in it. The psalmist paints a picture of the serenity of life as our Higher Power designed it to be.

Sadly, in human hands, God's harmonious design routinely gets corrupted. Unsatisfied with the natural abundance we have received, we push the earth's resources to depletion and exhaustion, interrupting God's delicate balance. We likewise seek to assert our self-will over those around us, destroying the harmony of loving human relationships.

It is the vision of God's creation in Psalm 104, where everything fits into a beautiful whole, that is the life our Higher Power wants for us. It is *why* he created us! As we learn to submit our will to his, we can begin to leave behind the chaos of our past and move toward peaceful harmony with the world around us.

All that God's creatures must do is look to him and follow his plan for their lives. When they do, God will "give them their food in due season; when you give to them, they gather it up; when you open your hand, they are filled with good things" (vv. 27–28).

God who made the moon to mark the seasons and taught the sun its time for setting, help us to find our rightful place in your glorious creation. May you grant us the serenity of a life lived in harmony with your will. Please keep us sober today.

Psalm 105

Seek the LORD and his strength;
  seek his presence continually.
Remember the wonderful works he has done,
  his miracles, and the judgments he has uttered.

(vv. 4–5)

We are presented in Psalm 105 with a short history of God's chosen people, from Abraham through Moses, and their arrival in the promised land. It is a story with its share of setbacks and suffering, a story that ultimately culminates in the joy and freedom of the life God always had in store for God's people.

Our own journeys through the slavery of addiction to the promised land of sobriety have a similar arc. There have been many times in my life when I, like the Hebrew people, grew weary and lost hope. Even after I quit drinking and began working the Twelve Steps, those promises of a sober life found on page 84 of the Big Book seemed extravagant indeed.

But God sends us help in the form of a recovery fellowship just as he sent his anointed leaders to help his ancient people. Our fellow alcoholics and addicts assure us that those promises, as the Big Book says, "will always materialize if we work for them" (p. 84). Their stories of recovery help us find the faith and determination we need until the promises begin to be fulfilled in our own lives, "sometimes quickly, sometimes slowly" (*Alcoholics Anonymous*, p. 84).

God kept his covenant with the Hebrew people, and he will keep his covenant with us, too. If we have faith and work the program set before us, we will enter into the joy and freedom of the promised land of sober living.

God, thank you for leading us out of the bondage and aimless wandering of addiction and into the promised land of sobriety. Please keep us sober today.

Psalm 106

Many times he delivered them,
> but they were rebellious in their purposes,
> and were brought low through their iniquity.
Nevertheless he regarded their distress
> when he heard their cry.

(vv. 43–44)

It has been said that to live is to suffer, and we often ask God to ease our pain. Sometimes, though, I imagine that God himself must know suffering greater than any I have experienced.

Psalm 106, like the psalm before it, recounts the early history of the covenant between God and God's chosen people. This time, though, the story turns on the people's failure to live up to their promise to follow God's will. It is a history of their repeated rebellion against God:

- They "rebelled against the Most High at the Red Sea" and "put God to test in the desert" (vv. 7–15).
- They became "jealous of Moses in the camp" (vv. 16–18).
- They "worshiped a cast image" at Horeb (vv. 19–23).
- They had "no faith in his promise" on arrival in their new land and followed the god Baal (vv. 24–31).
- "They angered the LORD at the waters of Meribah" and adopted other peoples' evil ways (vv. 32–39).

Time and again they broke God's heart, and yet, despite the pain he must have felt, "he regarded their distress when he heard their cry" and "showed compassion according to the abundance of his steadfast love" (vv. 44–45). How many times have we rejected God's will? How many times have we caused God to suffer? And yet, our Higher Power has never wavered in showing us love, never failed to offer us mercy and forgiveness. "Praise the LORD!" (vv. 1 and 48).

God of abundant love and infinite mercy, you have suffered endlessly on our account. Thank you for never turning your back on us when we fail to follow your will. Please keep us sober today.

Psalm 107

He brought them out of darkness and gloom,
    and broke their bonds asunder.
Let them thank the LORD for his steadfast love,
    for his wonderful works to humankind.
For he shatters the doors of bronze,
    and cuts in two the bars of iron.

(vv. 14–16)

I wept the first time I read Psalm 107. I was three-and-a-half months into recovery, and in these words, I found the deep truth of God's transforming power and redeeming love that had saved my life.

Psalm 107 is thought to be an expression of thanksgiving for God returning his people from exile back to the promised land. In verses 4–32, we encounter four short stories of struggle, desperation, and redemption. There are those lost in the desert (vv. 4–9), those imprisoned (vv. 10–16), those who were sick (vv. 17–22) and those caught in a storm at sea (vv. 23–32). In each story, the suffering fearful people "cried to the LORD in their trouble," and in each case, he saved them.

We learn by turns in Psalm 107 that God is the Higher Power who nourishes the hungry and thirsty (v. 9), breaks down the things that bind us (v. 16), heals the sick and delivers them from destruction (v. 20), and calms the sea and provides a safe haven (vv. 29–30).

God performs these miracles purely out of love for his suffering children. My tears flowed as I read these stories because I knew that God had performed just such a miracle in my own life when he broke away the chains of my addiction to alcohol. The full weight of God's redeeming love hit me in that moment, and I shed tears of joy and thanksgiving.

God, we cried out to you in our trouble and you brought us out of the utter darkness and broke away our chains. Thank you for your redeeming love. Please keep us sober today.

Psalm 108

I will give thanks to you, O LORD, among the peoples,
　and I will sing praises to you among the nations.
For your steadfast love is higher than the heavens,
　and your faithfulness reaches to the clouds.

(vv. 3–4)

It seems the question of will runs through the latter verses of Psalm 108. After a series of expressions of praise and thanksgiving, the psalmist seeks God's help with securing victory over the nation's enemies. In the final verses, he acknowledges an important truth: "Human help is worthless. With God we shall do valiantly; it is he who will tread down our foes" (vv. 12b-13).

Those of us in recovery might need to check our thinking a little more completely before we take the field of battle. As it says on page 62 of the Big Book of Alcoholics Anonymous, "the alcoholic is an extreme example of self-will run riot." Much of the work we must do early in our own program of recovery is intended to replace this extreme self-reliance with reliance on the God of our understanding. This can be very difficult. Even after we receive the desire to let our Higher Power call the shots, how are we supposed to know God's will?

The Big Book gives us a clue on page 63. As we begin to spend more and more time in God's presence, we become "less and less interested in ourselves, our little plans and designs" and more "interested in seeing what we could contribute to life." That is to say, we know we are acting in accordance with God's will when our first thought is for other people, not our own selfish interest.

God, we seek to live by your will, not our own. Help us to always think of others before ourselves, and please keep us sober today.

Psalm 109

Help me, O LORD my God!
  Save me according to your steadfast love.
Let them know that this is your hand;
  you, O LORD, have done it.

                   (vv. 26–27)

Alcoholism and addiction are often the subject of scorn and derision in our society. Rather than understanding and accepting that we suffer from a disease, we are often judged and criticized for what many see as a moral failing or weakness of the will. How many times did we hear, "Why don't you just stop? Why don't you drink like a normal person?"

If only it were that easy! In our frustration and shame, we can begin to feel angry and resentful toward our accusers, much as the author of Psalm 109 does. He is distraught by the unwarranted barrage of attacks on his character described in detail in verses 6–19. He seems to be trying to do the right thing, showing his enemies love and praying for them, but they just won't back off (vv. 3–4).

In such circumstances, it is natural to feel resentful and desire vengeance. The psalmist, though, turns to God. "Help me, O LORD my God! Save me according to your steadfast love" (v. 26). Certainly, a hint of revenge finds its way into his prayer, as he asks God to turn the tables on his enemies. But that kind of honest prayer is often important in letting go of a situation and giving it over to God.

When we honestly share our hurt and frustration with God, asking that he take control, we might not find our enemies punished the way we think they deserve. We will, however, find our serenity begin to flow back in as God helps us to let go of our anger and resentment.

God, we turn over to you the hurt, anger, and frustration we feel when we are wronged by others. Help us to let go and find the serenity that can only come from you. Please keep us sober today.

Psalm 110

The LORD sends out from Zion
  your mighty scepter.
  Rule in the midst of your foes.
                                (v. 2)

The royal psalms, such as Psalm 110, deal with themes of kingship, just rule, and the nation's challenges and victories. Kings often have chief ministers and other officials who carry out their plans and handle the daily tasks of ruling. Here, the king seems to be playing the role of chief minister to the God of his understanding, the one true ruler over all the earth. When the king and the nation are aligned with God and his will, good things will happen.

As so often is the case with the Psalms, we can see in Psalm 110 a metaphor for our personal lives. The poem begs the question, if we will entertain it, who is the ruler over our lives? Do we make ourselves the ruler, or are we God's chief ministers, following his will and putting his plans into motion?

As for most of us in recovery, my answer is a before-and-after story. Before I got sober, I heeded no wise counsel, relied on my own power, and sought my own selfish ends. Pain and suffering were the hallmark of my rule, and I ran my tiny "kingdom" into the ground. After I got sober, I began to understand I had no rightful claim to the throne. I pledged my allegiance to the God of my understanding as king over all and sought to do his bidding. Sometimes I am not the most obedient chief minister and still tend to substitute my judgment for God's. Fortunately, my king expects only my honest best effort and readily forgives my shortcomings.

God, you are our one true king. Help us to serve you better and follow your will, not our own. Please keep us sober today.

Psalm 111

Great are the works of the LORD,
   studied by all who delight in them.
Full of honor and majesty is his work,
   and his righteousness endures forever.
                          (vv. 2–3)

The question may arise for ourselves and others, why does recovery have to involve God? Why is it so important to embrace a program, a way of life, centered around spiritual principles instead of some other alternative? This is the question taken up in Psalm 111, and the psalmist bases his answer on the nature of God himself and the Word (or teachings) God has given us.

We can see the nature of God in his great works. Consider the words the poet uses to describe them: honor, majesty, righteousness, wonderful, gracious, merciful, faithful, and just. We can see that our Higher Power reveals his love and strength through what he does: "He provides food for those who fear him; he is ever mindful of his covenant. He has shown his people the power of his works, in giving them the heritage of the nations" (vv. 5–6).

God's teachings, the psalmist writes, reflect the character of their author. His "precepts are trustworthy" (v. 7) and are "established forever and ever" (v. 8). They are no sham, no passing fad, but a solid foundation for a better way of living. "The fear of the LORD," the psalmist tells us ("fear" meaning respect or reverence), "is the beginning of wisdom; all those who practice it have a good understanding" (v. 10). For those of us with a disease that causes us to misperceive the truth about ourselves and the world around us, what could be better?

God, you reveal yourself to be the source of all love, power, and knowledge. Help us to faithfully follow where you lead. Please keep us sober today.

Psalm 112

Praise the LORD!
　Happy are those who fear the LORD,
　　who greatly delight in his commandments.

　　　　　　　　　　　　　　　　(v. 1)

In the previous psalm, we read of the character of God and the goodness of his teachings. In Psalm 112, we have a meditation on what life is like for those who revere God and follow his will and way. Spoiler alert: Life is good!

In Psalm 111, the psalmist made the case that evidence of God's power and love comes not only from God's words but also God's works. So, in Psalm 112 we see that the righteous not only hear and respect God's teachings, but they also put them into action.

What does this "righteousness," or faithfulness to God, look like in practice? In verses 4–8, the psalmist describes their way of life:

- They are a light in the darkness.
- They are gracious and merciful
- They are generous and just.
- They are secure and steady.

Essentially, those who follow this program for living are committed to loving service to others above all else. God in turn rewards their good works with a happy life, free from fear, and full of God's abundance.

On page 89 of the Big Book of Alcoholics Anonymous, it says that "nothing will so much insure immunity from drinking as intensive work with another alcoholic." As with righteousness, sobriety is as much about what we do as what we know or believe. Loving service to others is our task, and sobriety is our reward.

God, give us the courage to put what you are teaching into action by helping others. Please keep us sober today.

Psalm 113

He raises the poor from the dust,
   and lifts the needy from the ash heap,
to make them sit with princes,
   with the princes of his people.
                       (vv. 7–8)

We are again called to praise in the opening line of Psalm 113, an introductory call it shares with the preceding two psalms. Here, our praise is to continue all day long, "from the rising of the sun to its setting" (v. 3). This same encouragement to offer praise to God, fittingly, also concludes Psalm 113, and in between the psalmist offers good reasons for God's worthiness for this praise-a-thon.

In verses 5 and 6, the psalmist asks, "Who is like the LORD our God, who is seated on high, who looks far down on the heavens and the earth?" We can assume this to be a rhetorical question, with the obvious answer that no one can compare to our Higher Power. More than just making a general statement about God's limitless power and goodness, though, the psalmist shares two examples of specific ways in which the God of our understanding uses power in uniquely praiseworthy ways: God "raises the poor from the dust, and lifts the needy from the ash heap" (v. 7) and "He gives the barren woman a home, making her the joyous mother of children" (v. 9). We could add another verse: He breaks the chains of addiction, and gives hope, peace, and freedom to the desperate.

In our society, it is the winners—the clever, the beautiful, the educated, the rich, the famous—who seem to get all the breaks. But the Higher Power we encounter in the Psalms is the God of the suffering, the hopeless, those yearning to be free. He harnesses his unrivaled power with even greater love to mend those who are broken and find his lost children. "Praise the LORD!"

God, thank you for loving those of us in need of your saving grace, whether the world thinks we deserve it or not. Please keep us sober today.

119

Psalm 114

Tremble, O earth, at the presence of the LORD,
  at the presence of the God of Jacob,
who turns the rock into a pool of water,
  the flint into a spring of water.

(vv. 7–8)

Another psalm that briefly recounts the exodus of God's people from Egypt to the promised land, Psalm 114 includes beautiful imagery testifying to God's great power. In verses 3 and 4, the sea flees, a river turns back, and the mountains and hills skip away like sheep in the face of the Almighty.

The psalm ends with perhaps the greatest example of God's power when the psalmist writes of water flowing from rocks at his command. The geographic setting for much of the Bible is a dry and arid land where water, the source of all life, is always in short supply. Water often appears in the Psalms as a symbol of God's ultimate power—the ability to give and sustain life.

At times, the water symbolism refers to God's granting of abundance in support of our physical and material needs. In other places, as in the Christian rite of baptism, it represents God's gift of spiritual life and renewal. Whether physical or spiritual, it is living water that sustains and redeems God's people.

How fitting for an alcoholic that this recurring symbol of God's love and life-giving power comes in liquid form! All of us sought liquid sustenance in alcohol, only to find more pain and suffering. Through the Twelve-Step program of recovery, however, our Higher Power will dump out the liquor and fill our cup with living water, quenching our spiritual thirst as nothing else ever could.

God, we wandered in the barren desert of our addiction, never able to quench our thirst. Thank you for your living water that has given us new life. Please keep us sober today.

Psalm 115

Our God is in the heavens;
   he does whatever he pleases.
Their idols are silver and gold,
   the work of human hands.

(vv. 3–4)

In the second of the Twelve Steps, we begin the process of building a relationship with a "Power greater than ourselves." This Higher Power, referred to in the Big Book as God, isn't defined or described in much detail, but is said to be a God "of our own understanding."

I believe the founders of AA used this expansive language about God so as not to exclude any religions or traditions. The focus of the program is on *spirituality*, not religious doctrine. At the same time, the Big Book encourages us to connect with a God of our own *understanding*, not of our own *creation*.

Psalm 115 helps us grasp the importance of this distinction. In verses 4–8, the psalmist describes the nature of gods that are "the work of human hands." He tells us such gods have no capacity to act and are like those who made them. In other words, they have no power greater than their human creators.

The Big Book says "there is one who has all power—that One is God. May you find him now!" (p. 59). This God certainly is understood differently by each of us, but he is a God more powerful than all of us, and a God we must *find*, not *create*. It is this God the psalmist describes as our help and our shield (v. 11), the God who is mindful of us and will bless us (v. 12).

All-powerful God, you are the creator of all that was, is, and ever shall be. May you continue to reveal yourself to us. Please keep us sober today.

Psalm 116

For you have delivered my soul from death,
  my eyes from tears,
  my feet from stumbling.
I walk before the LORD
  in the land of the living.

(vv. 8–9)

Once again, we find in Psalm 116 a story of God's saving grace that could have come from any of us who have suffered from addiction. "The snares of death encompassed me," the psalmist writes in verse 3. "O LORD, I pray, save my life," he cried out (v. 4), and God saved him when he was "brought low" (v. 6).

The outlines of my own story are very similar, and, like the psalmist, I found myself asking, "What shall I return to the LORD for all his bounty to me?" (v.12). How could I possibly repay God for the incredible gift of sobriety? In a certain sense, it is a gift that can never be repaid. There is really nothing we can do to *earn* God's grace. What we can do, as suggested in Psalm 116, is to "lift up the cup of salvation and call on the name of the LORD" (v. 13).

In essence, what the psalmist is telling us is that all God asks in return is for us to continue to live in grateful relationship to our Higher Power. What God wants more than anything, what he created each of us for, is to live in loving companionship with him.

This is not, however, a relationship of equals. God leads, we must follow. We must try to submit ourselves and deny our urge to take back control. This is sometimes difficult to do, but it becomes easier when we begin each day in conscious contact with the God of our understanding, remembering how we were saved from the "snares of death," and doing what we can to help others break free.

God, thank you for delivering our souls from death, our eyes from tears, our feet from stumbling. May we live into the loving relationship you desire for us. Please keep us sober today.

Psalm 117

Praise the LORD, all you nations!
   Extol him, all you peoples!
For great is his steadfast love toward us,
   and the faithfulness of the LORD endures forever.
Praise the LORD!

(vv. 1–2)

When a writer repeats an idea over and over, we can assume it is worth special attention. It is as if the author is saying, "Look, I know I've said this already, but I'm saying it again in case you missed it the first time. It's really important."

There are certainly such repeating messages in the Psalms, and none repeated more often in this section of the collection than the words that open and close Psalm 117: "Praise the LORD!" There is no question that the psalmists are trying to drive home this "praise" thing, but why is it so important? The author of Psalm 117, shortest of the Psalms, gives us a concise answer. We must praise God because his love and faithfulness never fail!

No matter what we've done—or failed to do—God will *always* love us. No matter how completely we may have let him down, God will never abandon us. When we are working a good program and staying near to God, God will stay near to us. And when we are not doing the things we should and neglecting our spirituality, still God is there.

God's unfailing love certainly deserves our praise. But we may find praising God also does something for us. When things are going well, it reminds us that it is our Higher Power's work, not ours, and helps us stay humble. When the going gets tough, praising God reminds us of all the good things we have received and how our Higher Power has sustained us through the storms of life. Praising God at any time is good for us every time.

We praise you, O God, for your steadfast love and enduring faithfulness. Thank you for always standing by us, in good times and in bad, whether we deserve it or not. Please keep us sober today.

Psalm 118

Out of my distress I called on the LORD;
   the Lord answered me and set me in a broad place.
With the LORD on my side I do not fear.
   What can mortals do to me?

(vv. 5–6)

Psalm 118 is a hymn of thanksgiving that flows from recognition of a fundamental characteristic of God: "His steadfast love endures forever" (vv. 1–4, 29). It is by God's steadfast love that the psalmist has been saved, and it is the source of his faith that God will sustain him in the future.

The psalmist offers testimony from his life that gives us a before-and-after picture of God's work. He writes that God has "set me in a broad place" (v. 5), which evokes the image of the "Broad Highway" described as the life of sobriety in the Big Book (pp. 55 and 75). Gone are the distress and fear that afflicted the psalmist when he felt his troubles "surrounded me like bees" (v. 12).

It is clear from the joy shining through in the poem that new life in the broad place of God is vastly better. Living on a spiritual basis has even made the psalmist feel useful again. In verse 22, he tells us "the stone that the builders rejected has become the chief cornerstone." We encounter this same promise of a useful life in the Big Book (p. 84) and throughout the *Twelve Steps and Twelve Traditions* (pp. 39, 53, 102, 111, 114, 121, 124).

What an amazing example of God's transforming love. We, who were not even able to manage our own lives, can become truly useful in sobriety, contributing to society and using our experience, strength, and hope to help others. Thanks be to God!

We thank you, God, for taking these rejected stones and using us to help build a better world. Please keep us sober today.

Psalm 119

Happy are those whose way is blameless,
  who walk in the law of the LORD.
Happy are those who keep his decrees,
  who seek him with their whole heart.
                      (vv. 1–2)

The longest of the Psalms (indeed, the longest chapter of the entire Bible), Psalm 119 is a masterwork of spiritual writing. In this intricately structured poem, we find an articulation of the core message of the entire book. In essence, it is an instruction manual for happy living, as we are told in the opening verses.

The words of Psalm 119 are the reflections of an individual striving to live a righteous life. By "righteous," both as it is used here and throughout the Psalms, I do not mean "perfect." The psalmist readily admits that he has gone astray (v. 176; see also vv. 67, 71, and 92). Righteousness instead consists of a ceaseless *effort* to learn and live by God's teachings. Such knowledge allows the psalmist to live in the peace of God's presence (v. 165), freed from the stresses and worries of life.

This understanding gained from constant meditation on God's teachings has practical implications for daily living. In an often-cited verse, the psalmist writes, "Your word is a lamp to my feet and a light to my path" (v. 105). It motivates the psalmist to act in accordance with God's will (vv. 59–60) and transforms him into God's servant (vv. 124–125). Living in harmony with God's word, however, does not make the psalmist immune from difficulty, as we see in his frequent mention of enemies and the trouble he encounters. He has learned, though, that his happiness depends on turning to God when the going gets rough (vv. 86, 94, 109–110, 146–147, 169–170).

All in all, Psalm 119 seems like a fairly complete blueprint for living.

God, we love your teachings. May we always seek to know you better, serve you each day, and turn to you for strength and comfort. Please keep us sober today.

Psalm 120

In my distress I cry to the Lord,
  that he may answer me:
"Deliver me, O Lord,
  from lying lips,
  from a deceitful tongue."
(vv. 1–2)

Feelings of alienation have played a big role in my disease. For much of my life, the sense that I was on the outside looking in stoked my fears and resentments, eroding my self-worth. I turned to alcohol, in part, because it freed me for a time from those anxieties, making me feel like I belonged. But the comfort never lasted. As the effects of alcohol ebbed away, the old anxieties would flow back in.

The author of Psalm 120 shares his own feelings of alienation, triggered by social and geographic isolation. He calls out to God because of the "lying lips" of those talking behind his back (v. 2). He feels like an "alien" in a foreign land, unable to relate to the people around him (vv. 5–6).

Sometimes these feelings of alienation cling to us in sobriety. In fact, they can get worse as we face broken relationships that are difficult—even impossible—to restore. Some of us end up in residential treatment programs where we are physically isolated from family and friends. It all can lead to feelings of loneliness that risk putting us on a path toward relapse.

Like the psalmist, we can turn to the God of our understanding for deliverance. We will find that our Higher Power has given us the gift of fellowship with others in recovery. When we go to recovery meetings, we will find ourselves surrounded by those who are facing the same challenges and fears. They will put flesh to God's promise that we will never again have to be alone.

God, sometimes we feel lonely and afraid. Help us to find comfort in the fellowship of recovery and please keep us sober today.

Psalm 121

I lift up my eyes to the hills—
    from where will my help come?
My help comes from the LORD,
    who made heaven and earth.
(vv. 1–2)

Early in my sobriety, I learned at AA meetings that a "real" alcoholic is someone who will never be able to master the art of controlled drinking. My own experience validated what I heard and read. Countless times I tried to cut back, and none of my clever ideas worked. I tried to drink only on certain days or after a certain time, tried to limit myself to two drinks or half a bottle, tried switching from liquor to wine or beer, tried only buying what I intended to drink that night. None of it worked.

What many alcoholics can't see until we get sober is that we suffer from a disease that created a mental obsession and physical craving for alcohol, our drug of choice. It isn't the second or sixth or tenth drink that gets us—it's the first. And we're told on page 43 of the Big Book of Alcoholics Anonymous that if we fail to maintain our spiritual condition, we will end up with no defense against that first drink. It will only be a matter of time, under those circumstances, before we relapse.

Psalm 121 issues a call to us to put our trust in a Higher Power, from whom our help will come (vv. 1-2). "The LORD," writes the psalmist, "is your keeper" (v. 5). He will "keep you from all evil; he will keep your life" (v. 7). All we must do is maintain our trust in God's power to defend us from that first drink, and we demonstrate that trust by staying in close daily contact with God. The psalmist assures us in verse 3 that God will never fall asleep at the wheel or take a day off. Neither can we.

God, thank you for never failing in your watchfulness over us. Help us to build our trust in your power by spending time with you each day. Please keep us sober today.

Psalm 122

"Peace be within your walls,
 and security within your towers."
For the sake of my relatives and friends
I will say, "Peace be within you."

(vv. 7–8)

Scholars believe the group of Psalms 120–134, each with the superscription "A Song of Ascents," might have been prayers or songs used by pilgrims as they climbed the streets up to the temple in Jerusalem for religious ceremonies and festivals. Psalm 122 celebrates that city as the dwelling place of the Most High, and the psalmist encourages his community to pray for God's hometown to be a place of peace.

In the world of human affairs, peace can be hard to come by. Competition for control and dominance seems to be the guiding principle for behavior in many of the institutions and organizations that constitute a large part of our social and working lives. The founders of Alcoholics Anonymous recognized that the fellowship they were forming needed to embrace a different ethic if it was to be a place of peace and refuge for the suffering alcoholic. "We alcoholics see that we must work together and hang together," it says in the introduction to AA's Twelve Traditions, "else most of us will finally die alone" (*Alcoholics Anonymous*, p. 561).

Most of the AA traditions, from the opening emphasis on unity and God as the ultimate authority, to the commitment to self-sufficiency and no permanent formal organizational structure, echo the psalmist's prayer: "Peace be within your walls" (v. 7). We all have a role to play in respecting these principles in our recovery fellowships so that others can find the same welcoming place of peace that helped start each of us on the road to recovery.

God, may we always keep our focus on you and the work of recovery so that all may find the peace and fellowship they need to get well. Please keep us sober today.

Psalm 123

As the eyes of servants
    look to the hand of their master,
as the eyes of a maid
    to the hand of her mistress,
so our eyes look to the LORD our God,
    until he has mercy upon us.

(v. 2)

Comfort for the mind and heart can be difficult to find. I often turned to alcohol, my drug of choice, to quiet the "demons," as I called them, those relentless feelings of anxiety that tormented me. The more I drank, though, the less effective alcohol became as a comforter—and my demons seemed to multiply.

The author of Psalm 123 has had "more than enough" of being troubled and downtrodden, and he cries out to God to have mercy on him and his community (v. 3). He casts the people as servants and maids begging for the one in authority to relieve their suffering. This imagery acknowledges an important truth: God is in control. Our Higher Power is benevolent and will lighten our burdens if we turn to him.

We may find relief to be elusive when we first get sober. We are likely grateful to not be drinking anymore, but those demons of the past never want to let us go. We find moments of peace here and there, but they just don't seem to last. Over time, we begin to realize that to get free of all those anxieties, we have to let God change us. The more we learn to hand control over to our Higher Power, the more serenity will flow into us. If we let the God of our understanding run the show, the comfort seems to come naturally.

Great Comforter, have mercy on us! We give you control over our lives. Please keep us sober today.

Psalm 124

Blessed be the LORD,
　who has not given us
　as prey to their teeth.
We have escaped like a bird
　from the snare of the fowlers;
the snare is broken,
　and we have escaped.

(vv. 6–7)

Our lives seem to hinge on a single question: God or no God? The answer we provide each day through our actions and the choices we make has profound implications. Indeed, it is the question and answer on which everything else depends.

Psalm 124 uses a powerful if/then structure to emphasize the importance of the "God question" and our lived response. The psalmist uses vivid imagery to set up the "if" and "then" of reliance on a Higher Power in the opening verses of the psalm. *If* his people had not chosen God as their hope and strength, *then* their enemies would have "swallowed us up alive" (v. 3) and "the flood would have swept us away" (v. 4).

The images of swallowing and flooding hits this alcoholic right between the eyes. My enemy, alcohol, was swallowing me whole as I swallowed drink after drink. I sometimes felt I was slowly drowning in a sea of booze. On my own, I was powerless to rescue myself, but this was not the end of my story.

As the psalmist describes in the closing verses, using the image of a bird flying free from a trapper's snare, a happy ending is in reach if we can answer the God question differently. *If* we turn to the God of our understanding and turn our will and our lives over to God's care, *then* we can be saved from our enemy and lifted out of the rising torrents of our disease. *Then* we can fly free into the open skies of sobriety.

God, we turn to you, knowing you have the power to save us from our enemy and set us free. Please keep us sober today.

Psalm 125

As the mountains surround Jerusalem,
  so the LORD surrounds his people,
  from this time on and forevermore.
For the scepter of wickedness shall not rest
  on the land allotted to the righteous,
so that the righteous might not stretch out
  their hands to do wrong.

(vv. 2–3)

There is a beautiful image in Psalm 125 of God protecting his people the way the surrounding mountains protect the holy city, Jerusalem (v. 2). There they reside in God's enduring company. Living in closeness with God, as the psalmist describes it, offers them an interesting sort of protection—against the harm they could do themselves by "stretch[ing] out their hands to do wrong" (v. 3).

Before I got sober, I used to seek out people who would tell me what I wanted to hear. From family members to bartenders, I would give them a partial version of the truth as I sought their validation of my self-pity and resentments. There was still a voice inside me that made me question some of my thoughts and actions, so I tried to quiet that voice with bad advice and ever more drinking. I orchestrated things to hear what I wanted so that I could justify doing what I wanted, and my life continued to fall apart as the voice of conscience faded away.

I believe that inner voice is our Higher Power speaking to us, and it sometimes tells us what we don't want to hear. It's a voice that demands total honesty and relentlessly calls us to do the next right thing. Like a journey over mountainous terrain, listening to God's voice can be difficult and require sacrifice. But on arrival in the sheltered valley of God's presence, we will find the precious gifts of the serenity and joy of a sober life.

God, grant us the courage to listen for your voice. It calls us to do the next right thing so that we might find your lasting peace. Please keep us sober today.

Psalm 126

May those who sow in tears
    reap with shouts of joy.
Those who go out weeping,
    bearing the seed for sowing,
shall come home with shouts of joy,
    carrying their sheaves.

(vv. 5–6)

The return of an exiled people to their homeland is the topic addressed poetically in Psalm 126. It is worth noting that the psalmist focuses not just on the physical act of "return," but on the more spiritual concept of "restoration." We can think of the encouragement we share with one another in recovery fellowships to "keep coming back" in the same way.

On the surface, this line is about our continued presence at recovery meetings. The point, however, is not to fill the chairs in the room. Behind the call to keep coming back is a strong belief in the restorative power of the Twelve-Step program. Newcomers might begin with a great deal of skepticism and reluctance. It can be overwhelming to face the proposition of the radical change the program suggests as the basis of our recovery. If we stay long enough, though, we begin to see how the lives of others in the room have turned around, and some genuine willingness takes root in our hearts.

This is the beginning of the restoration we seek. As we open ourselves gradually to the possibility of God's transforming power, God can begin to work on us. If we stick to it and let our Higher Power take the wheel, we certainly will like the results!

God of restoration, give us the courage to keep coming back, even when we don't want to. Open our hearts to the possibilities of your power to transform our lives. Please keep us sober today.

Psalm 127

Unless the LORD builds the house,
those who build it labor in vain.
Unless the LORD guards the city,
the guard keeps watch in vain.
(v. 1)

In the opening verse of Psalm 127, God is cast in the role of architect and builder. It recalls a gospel song with the chorus, "I'm working on a building . . . for my Lord." That song always seemed like a good description of what it's like to work a twelve-step program—building the structure that will house a sober life.

The psalmist tells us, though, that "unless the LORD builds the house, those who build it labor in vain" (v. 1). If we draw up the blueprint and do all the work on our own, the house will surely crumble. Left to our own devices, we're likely to build a McMansion, big and pleasing to the eye, but built too quickly and cheaply to last a lifetime.

I have built that kind of "house" before, only to watch it fall apart. God is a much better builder, starting out with a solid foundation—the teachings our Higher Power gives us in the Psalms or a twelve-step program. God builds our lives, one day at a time, making sure each brick is set firmly in just the right place before moving on to the next. God's work doesn't always meet our own impatient construction schedules, but, as the Big Book tells us, we will be amazed before the work is halfway through. The house God builds for us will stand through the storms of life. In it we will find peaceful rest, no longer to eat "the bread of anxious toil" (v. 2).

God, you are the master builder. Thank you for building us back up, brick by brick. Please keep us sober today.

Psalm 128

Happy is everyone who fears the LORD,
   who walks in his ways.
You shall eat the fruit of the labor of your hands;
   you shall be happy, and it shall go well with you.

                              (vv. 1–2)

In the previous psalm, we received a warning that our efforts will not produce good results unless God is in control. Psalm 128 shows us the other side of the coin: "Happy is everyone who fears the LORD, who walks in his ways" (v. 1).

This psalm gives us some insight into the saying, "First things first," that commonly hangs on the wall of Twelve-Step meeting rooms. In the first two verses, the psalmist explains that our happiness comes from our commitment to following God's will and way for our lives. Then in verses 3 and 4, he predicts that good things will happen for those who put God first.

This way of thinking about happiness and "first things" seems to contradict the messages we get from society about success, money, and material comfort. It helps me see that I had it backward for many years. I used to be convinced that achievement, and the money and social recognition that accompanied it, would bring me happiness. I led a life of "if only"—*if only* I could improve this, change that, have the next thing, *then* I would be happy.

That approach will never work. Instead, it will leave us feeling unfulfilled, restless, and resentful, fueling our addiction. When we begin trying to follow the "God first" formula in Psalm 128, we finally begin to find the happiness that only our Higher Power can offer. When we start with the God of our understanding, we start from a happy place. Everything else is just icing on the cake.

God, you are the source of all happiness in life. Help us to put you first in all that we do. Please keep us sober today.

Psalm 129

"The plowers plowed on my back;
  they made their furrows long."
The Lord is righteous;
  he has cut the cords of the wicked.

(vv. 3–4)

Many of us have been under the assault of our disease since very early in our lives. Perhaps we didn't begin drinking or using until sometime in adulthood, but we usually can trace to an early age the patterns of thinking that are the roots of our later addiction.

I began drinking to excess as a teenager, although I didn't become a daily drinker until many years later. I even went for long stretches in adulthood—years in fact—without a drink. But I was a "dry drunk" during these times, plagued by the same selfishness, dishonesty, and resentfulness that are defining features of my sickness.

In Psalm 129, the author writes of the trauma of being under constant attack since youth. "The plowers plowed on my back; they made their furrows long," he writes in verse 3. This poetic image suggests how deeply the seeds of addiction are planted within us, how those long furrows of our disease can be like scars on our backs. It is no easy task to uproot something so deeply planted, something that has grown and thrived for so long.

The psalmist appears to know enough about gardening to realize that once established, weeds tend to grow back quickly after you pull them. He turns to God for help, as we must, in wiping out these unwanted plants sewn by the enemy. Only with the strength and wisdom of the Master Gardener can our lives begin to bear the good fruit of recovery.

God, help us to uproot the weeds of addiction that have overgrown in our lives, planting in their place the new seeds of hope and freedom in the fertile soil of recovery. Please keep us sober today.

Psalm 130

Out of the depths I cry to you, O LORD.
  Lord, hear my voice!
Let your ears be attentive
  to the voice of my supplications!

(vv. 1–2)

To quote the late Tom Petty, "The waiting is the hardest part," and so it seems to be for the writer of Psalm 130, crying out for God to hear him.

It occurs to me that the psalmist's impatience could be motivated not only by his desire for things to get better, but also, in part, by his faith. He expresses confidence in verses 4 and 7 in God's forgiveness, love, and redeeming power, likely because he has experienced them before. He knows God can rescue him, so he is confident in his prayers.

For those of us who have tasted God's saving grace, this kind of impatience is only natural. We have first-hand knowledge of God's miraculous power, having witnessed his victory over alcohol and drugs in our lives. I sometimes wonder, if my Higher Power was able to set me free from addiction, what's taking him so long to help me with other, less daunting problems? Why won't God hurry up and act?

As we grow in recovery, we begin to realize that it is often our own thinking causing the delay. When we get impatient with God, we usually are focused on some external situation that isn't really ours to control. Our prayers for God's urgent intervention to fix things can cast God as an agent to do our bidding. This gets things exactly backward and slows down God's real work—changing us. When we pray instead for acceptance, God can get on with the truly transformative work in our lives, and often those external problems seem a lot less urgent.

God, grant us serenity to accept what we cannot change, courage to change what we can, and wisdom to know the difference. Please keep us sober today.

Psalm 131

O Lord, my heart is not lifted up,
   my eyes are not raised too high;
I do not occupy myself with things
   too great and too marvelous for me.
But I have calmed and quieted my soul,
   like a weaned child with its mother;
   my soul is like the weaned child that is with me.

(vv. 1–2)

Why did we have to suffer so long and cause so much pain for others? Why did we receive the gift of sobriety while others are dying from our disease? Why do bad things happen to good people while so many of the wicked prosper? Why?

If we allow ourselves to be tormented by such questions, our serenity is in jeopardy. I once had boundless confidence in the power of my own mind to work through any question, no matter how difficult. I refused to accept any proposition, including God's existence, unless I first answered all the hard questions to my own satisfaction. In other words, I was incapable of faith—in anything but myself.

The writer of Psalm 131 rejects this kind of arrogance. He has enough humility to say, "I do not occupy myself with things too great and too marvelous for me" (v. 1). He chooses instead to trust his Higher Power like a little child trusts its mother. He has faith, and from his faith comes acceptance; and from acceptance, peace.

When we focus on what we *do* know—that the God of our understanding freed us from the prison of addiction—we find the faith to accept that there are some things we just don't need to know, and our serenity tends to stick around.

God, may we let go of the questions that torment us and lean into you like a child nestles into its nurturing mother. Please keep us sober today.

Psalm 132

Rise up, O LORD, and go to your resting place,
    you and the ark of your might.
Let your priests be clothed with righteousness,
    and let your faithful shout for joy.

(vv. 8–9)

We encounter in Psalm 132 the retelling of a story of faithfulness and blessing, full of symbolism from Israel's history. King David, chosen by his Higher Power to lead his people, is making good on a long-standing promise to build a temple for God. The first step is the recovery of the ark of the covenant, which will be placed at the center of the temple.

The unfamiliar references to footstools, arks, and horns can be difficult to understand, and, therefore, easy to dismiss. At its heart, however, Psalm 132 is a story of God's blessing to David, followed by David's faithful response to God (vv. 1–10) and the promise of further blessings from God (vv. 11–18).

When we frame the story at this highest level, the psalm quickly becomes relevant to our journey of recovery. We receive an incredible blessing from God when he first makes us sober and removes from us our obsession with alcohol or drugs. We are then called to faithful response to this great gift by working the steps, improving our conscious contact with God and helping others. Our Higher Power then responds with even more blessings as we see the ninth-step promises (pp. 83-84 in the Big Book) come true in our lives. The vicious cycle of addiction is replaced with the virtuous cycle of recovery.

God, thank you for the many blessings you continue to bestow on us as we try to live in faithful response to the precious gift of sobriety. Please keep us sober today.

Psalm 133

How very good and pleasant it is
when kindred live together in unity!
(v. 1)

As a newcomer, one of the things I liked least about AA meetings was all the people. That might sound terrible, but it was the truth. An introvert by nature, I found the idea of walking into a room full of strangers to be a scary proposition. I even put off getting a sponsor for some time out of sheer social discomfort, entertaining the idea that Jesus could be my sponsor, and I could work the program on my own.

So, the celebration of togetherness and unity that opens Psalm 133 is not a message that resonated with me the first time I read it. As with other elements of AA that made me uncomfortable in the beginning, though, God gave me just enough strength to overcome my social anxiety and keep coming back. I eventually worked up the courage to ask someone to be my sponsor and found a few meetings where I felt especially at ease. This was only possible because my fear of drinking again was greater than my social discomfort.

I thank God every day that he gave me the strength to stick with it. In time, I came to experience the great blessings of community the writer of Psalm 133 describes as anointing oil (v. 2) and dew on the mountainside (v. 3). I now am blessed with a sponsor who is a true friend, helping me through the ups and downs of my recovery journey. When I walk into my home group meeting, I have the feeling of being among "kindred," and I benefit each week as we share our experience, strength, and hope with one another. It turns out that sobriety is a team sport.

God, thank you for the blessing of the recovery community and the realization that we don't have to do this alone. Please keep us sober today.

Psalm 134

Come, bless the LORD, all you servants of the LORD,
    who stand by night in the house of the LORD!
Lift up your hands to the holy place,
    and bless the LORD.

(vv. 1–2)

The final Song of Ascents, Psalm 134 is addressed to "all you servants of the LORD" (v. 1). If we are taking seriously the program of Alcoholics Anonymous, then we must surely be among those to whom the psalmist is speaking. As the Big Book says on page 89, "nothing will so much insure our immunity from drinking as intensive work with other alcoholics."

If that strong statement isn't enough to propel us into service work, then we might consider another fact. In chapter 5, "How It Works," we get an overview of the entire program and an explanation of steps one through four. Chapter 6, "Into Action," covers steps five through eleven. The authors then spend all of chapter 7, "Working with Others," explaining the importance and techniques of twelfth-step service work. Some of this disparity in length could be justified by the complexity of step twelve, but the intensive focus on serving others also seems to flow from the passage quoted above. Nothing else we can do will strengthen our own sobriety more than helping another suffering from addiction.

Early in recovery, we might feel we have little to offer, but nothing could be further from the truth! We can't help someone work the steps if we haven't worked them ourselves. But can we welcome another newcomer to a meeting? Can we make coffee? Can we give someone a ride? Can we listen? With God's help, we can!

God, we want to be your servants. Use us however you see fit to help others suffering from our disease. Please keep us sober today.

Psalm 135

Your name, O Lord, endures forever,
    your renown, O Lord, throughout all ages.
For the Lord will vindicate his people,
    and have compassion on his servants.

(vv. 13–14)

Psalm 135 opens and closes with a call to praise and worship the God of the Psalms. In between, the psalmist provides the reasons why such praise is justified:

- God is all-powerful (vv. 5–7);
- God rescued the people from slavery in Egypt and gave them their own land (vv. 8–12);
- God will always take care of his people (vv. 13–14); and
- Other gods aren't up to the task (vv. 15–18).

Once again, we can see how we alcoholics and addicts have a lot in common with the ancient Hebrew tribes. An all-powerful God rescued us from slavery to alcohol and drugs, established us in the new land of sobriety, and continues to sustain us in recovery when other "gods" cannot. I think it is worth a moment to reflect on verses 13–14, as the action in Psalm 135 seems to hinge on these verses. Before them, the psalmist evokes the memory of what God has done for us. After them we read a sort of warning that we will not fare as well if we trust in anything or anyone else.

If I had to boil this all down to a simple statement, I would say, "Only God." It is God alone who is worthy of praise and trust because only God could save us from our disease—and only God can keep us sober today. In calling us to praise God, the psalmist is calling us to remember what the central truth of our lives in sobriety must be. Nothing else will do.

Only you, God, only you. Please keep us sober today.

Psalm 136

O give thanks to the God of gods,
  for his steadfast love endures forever.
O give thanks to the Lord of lords,
  for his steadfast love endures forever.

(vv. 2–3)

As the psalmist recounts the story of God's creation of all that exists and God's deliverance of the Hebrew people from slavery to the promised land, he repeats the same words in the second half of each of Psalm 136's twenty-six verses. This is the big "why" of God's actions and the central reason for our praise: "For his steadfast love endures forever."

This psalm was likely used in worship ceremonies as a call and response, with a leader reading aloud the first half of each verse, and the congregation replying in unison with the second. As I imagine this ancient scene, I can almost hear the voices of the people building in praise to God with each successive repetition until they are nearly shouting the words at the end, arms raised above their heads, tears streaming down their faces.

I don't know if that is how it really played out, but the image matches the feeling I get as I read Psalm 136, which I like to do out loud. It also makes me feel like I share in the heritage of countless souls across the centuries who have seen God's wondrous works and experienced God's steadfast love.

I like to imagine another scene: The people gathered at a recovery meeting each take a turn sharing something God has done in their lives. After each person speaks, everyone else responds together, "For his steadfast love endures forever." How beautiful a celebration that would be! Think today about what you would say when it was your turn to share and imagine everyone around you responding with resounding confirmation of God's enduring love.

We give thanks to you, God, for you are good. Your steadfast love endures forever! Please keep us sober today.

Psalm 137

By the rivers of Babylon—
   there we sat down and there we wept
   when we remembered Zion.
On the willows there
   we hung up our harps.

(vv. 1–2)

In Psalm 137, we find a song of mourning sung by a people who have suffered a great tragedy. The psalm opens with a scene of the humiliations endured by a people now living in the country of their captors, having lost their homeland and possessions to invading armies. The poem ends with a cry for vengeance that is shocking in its brutality, calling for the children of the enemy to be violently murdered.

The ugliness of this imagery leads some people to avoid Psalm 137 altogether. Part of what makes the psalter so beautiful and useful as a spiritual tool, however, is its unflinching embrace of the full range of human emotion, even those feelings we don't like to admit we have. The desire for revenge—perhaps less extreme in most cases than wishing for the brutal murder of our enemies' children—is likely familiar to us all. We learn from Psalm 137 that we can express even the most unholy of thoughts to God.

If we hold such negativity inside, it can eat away at us, tearing down our serenity and building up our resentments and self-pity. If we keep it locked up long enough, it can begin to poison our relationships and jeopardize our sobriety. The first step in letting go of such destructive emotions is being honest with the God of our understanding. As the Big Book of Alcoholics Anonymous says, "we claim spiritual progress rather than spiritual perfection" (p. 60). And progress can be difficult unless we can be honest about where we are.

God, we sometimes have thoughts and feelings we're not proud of. Help us feel comfortable sharing them honestly with you so that you can show us a better way. Please keep us sober today.

Psalm 138

The LORD will fulfill his purpose for me;
    your steadfast love, O LORD, endures forever.
Do not forsake the work of your hands.

(v. 8)

I recall the time I attended a church service about a week after I quit drinking. I felt entirely unworthy of being in the presence of God. I had previously rejected God's very existence. I had lived a life focused entirely on selfish desire and personal ambition. I had repeatedly harmed those who loved me most as I fell ever deeper into the pit of alcoholism.

I felt I had no right to walk through the doors of that church, but my longing for God's help overcame my fear and shame. So, in I went. What I found there amazed me. No judgment, no rejection. Only a warm welcome from those in attendance and a message of hope. I began coming back each week and eventually made it my church home. After attending for a few months, the pastor asked me to lead the responsive readings and the Scripture one Sunday. He knew I was an alcoholic and had just heard the ugly truth of my fifth step, my confession of personal wrongdoings. And still, he asked me.

As I stood before the congregation that morning reading from the Bible, I had to fight back tears. I felt the full power of a verse from Psalm 138 wash over me: "For though the LORD is high, he regards the lowly" (v. 6). No matter what we have done, we are not beyond the reach of God's saving grace. No matter what good works we may do in the future, we cannot earn God's favor. For that great gift, joining with the psalmist, "I give you thanks, O LORD, with my whole heart" (v. 1).

Though we walk in the midst of trouble, though we can never deserve your grace, you stretch out your hand of love to rescue us. Thank you, God! Please keep us sober today.

Psalm 139

If I take the wings of the morning
   and settle at the farthest limits of the sea,
even there your hand shall lead me,
   and your right hand shall hold me fast.
                    (vv. 9–10)

God is presented to us in Psalm 139 as omniscient (all-knowing) and omnipresent (everywhere at once). The psalmist acknowledges that God knows his every thought, movement, and deed (vv. 1–6). He asks, "Where can I go from your spirit? Or where can I flee from your presence?" (v. 7), before admitting that God cannot be evaded.

What to make of these unchanging qualities of God? On the one hand, it can be somewhat unnerving when we realize there is no hiding from God. There have been those moments when I have thought about taking a drink and said to myself, "No one will know." (Of course, if I truly accept that even one drink will plunge me back into heavy drinking, as I do, then everyone would know eventually.) Even in that moment of decision, though, I have felt my Higher Power's eyes upon me, aware that he was watching me closely. God would know the instant that poisonous cup touched my lips, and his heart would break.

Here's the great part of God walking with me every step of every day: divine strength is always on tap. In moments of weakness, doubt, and fear, infinite power is just a simple prayer away. Toward the end of Psalm 139, the author, having reminded himself of God's intimate familiarity with him and constant presence, leans into God's power to strengthen him in the face of trouble and lead him "in the way everlasting" (v. 24). May we follow his example.

God, we are never hidden from you, never far away. When our thoughts stray or our feet stumble, may we lean into your strength to refocus us and straighten our path. Please keep us sober today.

Psalm 140

I know that the LORD maintains the cause of the needy,
    and executes justice for the poor.
Surely the righteous shall give thanks to your name;
    the upright shall live in your presence.

                            (vv. 12–13)

A personal plea to God for deliverance and protection dominates
Psalm 140. The psalmist fears the plots of "evildoers" who seek
his downfall, and so he turns to God for help. As he does, he
expresses faith, both in God's ability and proclivity to save him.

We see in the final two verses that the basis for the psalmist's
confidence is identity—his God's and his own. He says that he
knows God is a God of love and justice who helps the poor and
needy. As a poor and needy person, in contrast to his "arrogant"
enemies, the writer does not doubt that God will protect him. As
a "righteous" and "upright" person, he has the expectation of living in God's presence (v. 13).

Again, we see the pattern of the *covenant*—the agreement or
mutual promise—God enters with his people. God agrees to sustain us with love and strength. We agree to stay humble and rely
on God's grace rather than our own power or selfish desire. If it
ever feels like the deal isn't working out for us, self-examination
usually reveals that we are the ones who haven't kept up our end
of the bargain. If we want God to help bear our burdens, we have
to give him the space to get a good grip on our lives.

*God, we are just poor and needy human beings who need your
help. May we always give you the space you need to work in our
lives. Please keep us sober today.*

Psalm 141

Set a guard over my mouth, O LORD;
   keep watch over the door of my lips.
Do not turn my heart to any evil,
   to busy myself with wicked deeds
in company with those who work iniquity;
   do not let me eat of their delicacies.

                                   (vv. 3–4)

At the end of each of our prayers in this book, we humbly ask that God would keep us sober today. Verse 3 of Psalm 141 offers what could be seen as a poetic version of that prayer, asking our Higher Power to guard our mouths and keep watch over our lips. Arguably, the psalmist is referring more to what might come out of his mouth than what he might put in it, but so are we.

When we ask God to keep us sober, we are certainly asking him to give us the strength to not drink or use. Avoidance of alcohol and drugs, though, is so urgent, so important precisely because of the destructive effect it would have on us and those around us. Our prayer, then, is as much about living a better life as it is about not drinking. We ask for God's protection from the impulses associated with our disease so that we can live into the sober, happy life he wants for each one of us.

This short, simple prayer for God to keep us sober is also a daily remembering of the first three steps of the Twelve-Step program. We acknowledge our powerlessness, turn to a power greater than ourselves, and do our best to embrace God's will and way. Our prayers don't have to be as beautiful and poetic as the words of Psalm 141 to be filled with meaning and power. In the five simple words, "please keep us sober today," we express everything we could ever really hope to receive from God.

God, we call upon you to be our refuge. Do not leave us defenseless against our enemy, but instead grant us one more daily reprieve. Please keep us sober today.

Psalm 142

Give heed to my cry,
    for I am brought very low.
Save me from my persecutors,
    for they are too strong for me.
Bring me out of prison,
    so that I may give thanks to your name.

(vv. 6–7a)

Toward the end of Psalm 142, the psalmist uses imagery of imprisonment to describe the problems he asks God to help him solve. I have often thought of my addiction as a prison, albeit one of my own making. I had lost my freedom of choice, no longer able to turn away from alcohol or live the way I wanted. Only by the grace of God did I avoid *actual* imprisonment as a consequence of my drunkenness, a fate many of us alcoholics and addicts endure eventually.

In thinking about alcoholism as a prison, we are able to see sobriety as a gift of new freedom. At first, we tend to focus on being free *from* old things. In sobriety we are free from our obsession with alcohol and drugs, which in turn frees us from all those consequences that followed—poor health, broken relationships, lost jobs, wasted money, trouble with the law, and the like.

Over time, however, we find that there is another side to God's freedom. Not only are we free *from*, we are free *to*, and this is what I believe the psalmist may be hinting at when he asks for freedom "so that I may give thanks to your name."

And how do we thank God? In prayer, yes, but also—and perhaps more importantly—through our actions. God frees us *from* our addiction and all the bad that comes with it so that we are free *to* live a happy, peaceful, useful life in sobriety. As sober, faithful people, we are free to love, free to help, free to give, free to enjoy, free to thrive. That is how we thank God.

Thank you, God, for freeing us from the prison of our addiction and freeing us to live a sober, happy, peaceful, useful life. Please keep us sober today.

Psalm 143

I remember the days of old,
   I think about all your deeds,
   I meditate on the works of your hands.
I stretch out my hands to you;
   my soul thirsts for you like a parched land.

(vv. 5–6)

The theme of faithfulness—both God's and the psalmist's—runs through Psalm 143. The "action" of this prayer turns on some personal difficulty the author has encountered. "For the enemy has pursued me," he writes in verse 3, "crushing my life to the ground, making me sit in darkness like those long dead."

In the face of this trouble, the psalmist implores God to be faithful and merciful, recalling God's great works of the past. The psalmist even asks God not to judge him harshly, implying he might not be entirely innocent in the situation he faces.

In verse 10, the author adds another form of faithfulness to the mix: his own faithfulness to God. He writes, "Teach me to do your will, for you are my God. Let your good spirit lead me on a level path." The verse embodies a sentiment similar to that behind the third and eleventh steps of the Twelve-Step program. By the time we find ourselves in recovery, we have realized, perhaps like the psalmist, that doing things our own way hasn't worked out extremely well. By making the decision to turn our will over to God, we seek a better way.

Rarely does this result in an overnight change. Being faithful to God, however, doesn't entail perfection. We won't always get it right, no matter how many years of sobriety we have. A faithful response to failure is characterized by willingness to examine our own actions, admit our wrongs, and recommit ourselves to God's will and way for our lives. If we remain open, God will continue to teach us, turning our weakness into strength.

God, you know better. When we stumble and fall, we pray that you will pick us up and put us back on your level path. Please keep us sober today.

Psalm 144

May our barns be filled,
   with produce of every kind;
may our sheep increase by thousands,
   by tens of thousands in our fields,
   and may our cattle be heavy with young.
May there be no breach in the walls, no exile,
   and no cry of distress in our streets.
                                        (vv. 13–14)

The author of Psalm 144 is dreaming of the good life. The references he makes to enemies and conflict suggest he might be living through a rough patch, but he calls on God, his rock, to help him overcome these challenges (vv. 5–8). He says that he will "sing a new song" to the God who will grant him victory and deliver him from his adversaries. Then the psalmist does an amazing thing. Amid his current difficulty, presumably before his Higher Power has rescued him, he dares to dream big, and is bold enough to share this imagined future with God, expressing faith that God will turn the vision into reality.

Sometimes, in the crush of problems, it is difficult to see beyond the present. The more we focus on the negative, the more likely we are to go into "why me" self-pity mode. Our serenity begins to crumble if we fall into this trap, making us crabby and restless.

Faith, as we see in Psalm 144, is the perfect antidote, not least because it tends to bring along its twin, vision. When we look to the God of our understanding and recall God's love and power, we are reminded that this, too, shall pass. When we are confident that our Higher Power can and will deliver us from whatever difficulties we currently face, our thoughts begin to turn toward a brighter tomorrow. With the psalmist, we can say expectantly, "Happy are the people whose God is the LORD" (v. 15).

God, we know you love us and have the power to carry us through any trouble we face. Help us keep our eyes locked on the abundant life you have in store for us. Please keep us sober today.

Psalm 145

They shall speak of the glory of your kingdom,
and tell of your power,
to make known to all people your mighty deeds,
and the glorious splendor of your kingdom.
(vv. 11–12)

Many of the psalms are petitions or pleas, personal and collective, for God to intervene. Here in Psalm 145, we find the words of someone on the other side of God's saving grace who is determined to share the good news with others. "Great is the LORD, and greatly to be praised," the psalmist writes in verse 3, adding, "One generation shall laud your works to another" (v. 4). He goes on to do just that, spending the remainder of the psalm celebrating the wonderful things God has done. But what is the point of singing God's praises publicly?

One big reason, found in verse 12, is "to make known to all people [God's] mighty deeds." We are told in the twelfth step that we are to carry our message to others who suffer so that they might also find the power of God that saved our lives. I am constantly amazed at the endless stream of new people walking into recovery meetings. Every time I lead a meeting, share in discussion, or shake a newcomer's hand, I can make known my Higher Power's mighty deeds. By telling others what the God of my understanding has done in my life, someone else might find a little hope and willingness to begin his or her own journey of recovery.

Each time I do this, I am always amazed at how it gives me new strength and opens the door for God to continue my ongoing transformation. That alone is a compelling reason to sing God's praises.

God, through your power and saving grace, we have been blessed with a new life in sobriety. May we boldly share that good news with others so that they can find you, too. Please keep us sober today.

Psalm 146

Do not put your trust in princes,
  in mortals, in whom there is no help.
When their breath departs, they return to the earth;
  on that very day their plans perish.

(vv. 3–4)

The final five psalms, 146–150, serve as a "doxology," or concluding hymns of praise, to the entire book. Each of these psalms expresses praise and thanksgiving for God's love, power, and character. After beginning with the same words that open each of those five psalms, "Praise the Lord!", Psalm 146 presents us with a clear choice regarding where to place our faith.

The psalmist encourages us not to put our trust in humans, even the mightiest among us, "in whom there is no help" (v. 3). Their strength does not endure, and "their plans perish" (v. 4). The only viable alternative is to put our faith in a Higher Power, and the psalmist offers some compelling reasons in the following verses why this is a good choice:

- God will always be there for us and takes special care of those who are down and out.
- God sets us free and opens our eyes.
- God is eternal.

When presented this way, the choice becomes obvious for me. I choose God!

Whether we look at our own lives or to the stories of others, we can see some solid evidence for the psalmist's claims. How many times have we been disappointed by other human beings? How many times have we, in turn, let other people down? Yet the God of our understanding has delivered what they, and we, could not. Yes, the choice is an easy one. Praise the Lord, indeed!

God, we give you praise and thanks for doing for us what mere humans never could. Please keep us sober today.

Psalm 147

His delight is not in the strength of the horse,
    nor his pleasure in the speed of a runner;
but the Lord takes pleasure in those who fear him,
    in those who hope in his steadfast love.
                             (vv. 10–11)

The God revealed in Psalm 147 contradicts some of our core social assumptions about winners and losers. In our society, good fortune seems to favor the bold, those who take the proverbial bull by the horns and emerge victorious. In business, politics, or sports, we celebrate the winners and forget the losers.

As Psalm 147 tells us, the God of the Psalms employs a different value system. God's attention, concern, and power flow not to those on top of the heap, but to the outcasts, brokenhearted, and downtrodden. He gathers them together, binds up their wounds and lifts them up (vv. 2–3, 6). This divine value system has important implications for God's expectations for his people. The psalmist explains in verses 10–11 that God isn't looking for strength and speed. Instead, "the Lord takes pleasure in those who fear him, in those who hope in his steadfast love." In other words, he is looking for followers, not leaders. With God, life is not a competition.

This lesson, welcome as it is, has not been an easy one for me to learn. I embraced at an early age the desire to be the best, constantly comparing and measuring myself against the achievements of others. This way of thinking made me proud in success and resentful in failure. It led me to a profoundly selfish focus in my life and contributed significantly to my drinking.

That's not the life my Higher Power wants for me. He loves me right here, right now, just the way I am. I cannot earn or deserve God's favor, but he gives it to me anyway. All I must do is accept it and follow him.

God, help us to stop the competition and accept the love you freely give. May we follow your will for our lives and put our hope in your power, not our own. Please keep us sober today.

Psalm 148

Praise him, sun and moon;
   praise him, all you shining stars!
Praise him, you highest heavens,
   and you waters above the heavens!
Let them praise the name of the LORD,
   for he commanded and they were created.
                                             (vv. 3–5)

There is a universal call in Psalm 148 that goes out to all creation to praise God. Heavenly beings and bodies, forces and creatures of nature, and all people are included in this call to praise the Most High. The expansiveness of the scope implies an important truth about God's dominion: It is without limit. He is the creator of all that exists, and everything is under his power and care.

I can sometimes fall into the trap of putting God in a box. I can end up, often subconsciously, treating some aspects of life as "God things," while I put others in a non-God category. There are spiritual things, like AA, church, and daily prayer time, and then there is "normal" life. But the Twelve Steps and the teachings of the Psalms tell me I must live life—all of life—on a spiritual basis. The twelfth step says I should seek to practice these principles in *all* my affairs.

God wants all of us, and as a friend is fond of saying, "All means all, and that's all it means." When we fail to acknowledge the expansive claim God makes on our lives, we sell ourselves short. We give God control of some things and retain power over others for ourselves. The problem is that our limited power will always deliver results inferior to what a Higher Power could achieve if only we open the door.

Our addiction is likely the biggest problem any of us have ever faced, but our Higher Power is up to the challenge. Imagine what God can do with the rest of us!

Praise you, O God! You are in all and rule over all, and there is no box that can contain you. May we open our entire lives to you. Please keep us sober today.

Psalm 149

Let the faithful exult in glory;
  let them sing for joy on their couches.
Let the high praises of God be in their throats
  and two-edged swords in their hands.

(vv. 5–6)

In Psalm 149, the psalmist makes clear that a committed relationship to a Higher Power carries with it both rewards and responsibilities. The first half of this hymn of praise is a celebration of God's gifts of life, joy, and freedom. The second half, shrouded in militaristic imagery (not to be taken literally), encourages God's people to join in the work of furthering justice and righteousness in the world.

Every one of us in recovery is a recipient of God's great gift. None of us would be the people we have become—indeed, many of us would not be alive—but for the miraculous gift of sobriety. Like the ancient Israelites, we owe our very existence to the intervention of a loving, powerful God, and together we offer our praise.

Psalm 149 also speaks to the task our Higher Power has set before us. I like the image of praise in verse 6 as a "two-edged sword." Praising God benefits us because it reminds us of all God has done for us. It is God's power, not our own, on which our sobriety depends. Our praise also can be a testimony to others. As we tell our stories, we can help other people realize there is no problem too great for God's power and give them hope for a better tomorrow by living on a spiritual basis. As we sing God's praises, in private and in public, new blessings materialize in our lives *and* in the lives of others. This is indeed "glory for all his faithful ones" (v. 9).

God, all praise to you! Thank you for the miraculous gift of sobriety. May we faithfully execute the task of helping others find you. Please keep us sober today.

Psalm 150

Let everything that breathes praise the LORD!
Praise the LORD!

(v. 6)

The ending to the book of Psalms couldn't be more fitting. As I explained in the preface, I had been drawn to the Psalms at various times in my life. They called to me again when I first got sober, and I began to read one psalm each day. This was a life-changing journey for me, as I hope it has been for you.

As we move through the Psalms, something very interesting can happen along the way. Through these ancient texts, we find the tools to build a relationship with the God of our own understanding. We come to know the creator of all, the all-powerful God for whom nothing is impossible. The God whose steadfast love endures forever, who heard us cry out from the utter darkness of the pit we had dug for ourselves. The God who, with infinite mercy, lifts us up and sets us free from the prison of addiction. This is the God who gives us the miraculous gift of sobriety, leading us forward one day at a time and restoring our souls.

This same God continues to bless us with new life, new hope, new strength, new joy, and new peace. Our Higher Power has begun teaching us his will and way that we might find the fullness of the life he has in store for us. God has again made us useful, granting us the task of helping those who suffer, through our words and deeds, so that they might find God, too.

At the end of the book of Psalms, we are greeted with joy. We can now understand more clearly the opening verses of Psalm 1, "Happy are those" whose "delight is in . . . the LORD." And while we may have come to the end of the Psalms, we are only at the beginning of this amazing journey of recovery.

"Let everything that breathes praise the LORD! Praise the LORD!"

Praise you, O God! You have brought us so far, and you are only getting started. We look forward to every step, every day with you as we trudge together this happy journey of recovery. Please keep us sober today.

Works Cited

Alcoholics Anonymous, 4th ed. New York: Alcoholics Anonymous World Services, Inc., 2001.

The Four Absolutes. Cleveland: Cleveland Central Committee of Alcoholics Anonymous, n.d.

The Twelve Steps and Twelve Traditions. New York: Alcoholics Anonymous World Services, Inc., 1981.

God can & will protect us,
God is a safe refuge, safe
haven "a hiding place."
    Past (some of the talk is from
perspective of sobriety; having
prayed, worked the steps, attend
mtgs, serve others) and some
interpretations speak from what we
can do ... seek God's protection

            What it used to be like _
What happened? & What it is now?
    We can't; God can.
Thankful [have gratitude] for the things
God is doing for us _
        "TAKE IT TO THE LORD
IN PRAYER."
            Act of talking to God.

- "addiction in parking lot doing push-ups."
- SOBER "Son of a bitch it's Everything is real
- live life on life's terms
- God's time is ones day at a time, time
- Ps. 14 fools say "There is no God!"
- We don't have to do this alone.
- AA 4 absolutes: honesty, unselfessness, love and purity"
- Respond to God by doing his will.
- Ps 16 Those who choose another God multiply their sorrows.

LET GO OF THE OLD IDEA THAT WE ARE IN CONTROL Honestly & fully embrace God's will

Ps. 20 reassuring